The
Purpose
of
Life

T0290796

Find Your Path to
Oneness

HARIT RATNA

FiNGERPRINT!

Published by

FiNGERPRINT!

An imprint of Prakash Books India Pvt. Ltd

113/A, Darya Ganj,
New Delhi-110 002
Email: info@prakashbooks.com/sales@prakashbooks.com

 Fingerprint Publishing
 @FingerprintP
 @fingerprintpublishingbooks
www.fingerprintpublishing.com

ISBN: 978 93 6214 412 6

Acknowledgment

I extend my heartfelt thanks to all those whose invaluable contributions played a pivotal role in bringing this book to fruition.

Firstly, I wish to convey my deepest love to Mother Nature and my Guru for the invaluable gift of wisdom that infuses every word of this manuscript.

A special appreciation goes to Falguni Jain for her profound engagement with the manuscript, refining it to meet the standards expected by publishers.

I doff my hat to Anindam Dutta, the HueNi Studios team, and Sanjay Sharma at Balaji Graphics for their outstanding visualization of the book's ideas. Their contributions played a significant role in capturing publishers' attention and bringing the draft to life.

I express my deepest gratitude to Shantanu Dattagupta, Executive Publisher, Prakash and Fingerprint Books, for wholeheartedly supporting and providing a splendid platform for this work. I commend Shruti Tiwari for her unwavering dedication and sincere exploration of history and philosophy, shaping a book that I believe will withstand the test of time. I marvel at the sheer brilliance of Gavin Morris and the design team at Prakash for weaving a canvas that gives this book's content a magnificent stage.

Scope of Work

This book serves as a compendium of Frequently Asked Questions regarding the pursuit of conscious growth, often referred to as spiritual, personal, or inner development. It is my aspiration that these profound inquiries, alongside their clarifications, will illuminate your journey towards higher consciousness.

This book is dedicated to the Universe for
her unconditional love and to my
Oneness family for their boundless energy.

Contents

Introduction

What is consciousness?

Most people believe that the word refers to our state of awareness of our surroundings. More specifically, consciousness is considered to be the capacity to make sense of our reality and leverage our understanding to forge a connection with our environment. Let us take an example.

You are about to throw a piece of metal—a disc—into a drain, which is located at a distance. You know the object is hard. You know that it could hurt someone if they came in the way. You are also aware that if that person is harmed, you would face legal action. Furthermore, you see a person approaching the drain. To ensure their safety, you wait for them to pass. Once they are gone, you decide to chuck the disc.

How did your mind arrive at this decision? You drew inferences from the information that you gathered from the environment. Then, you made a decision based on the conclusions. Your decision was driven by an awareness of your objective reality—the laws of science, ethics, values of society, etc.—layered on your physical observations. This is the idea of consciousness prevalent in society—information about the 3D (sensory) world with a coat of reasoning. This view of consciousness, however, is extremely limited because it does not capture its multidimensional essence.

Our objective reality is limited to only what we can experience through the five senses—sight, smell, sound, touch, and taste. Therefore, consciousness, as it is commonly understood, is restricted to the data we collect through our sensory organs. However, there are other inputs that we glean from the environment via means that are not our five biological senses. For instance, we use a non-biological sense—our conscience—to relay an inner voice that guides us toward our value system. Conscience helps us to decode non-sensory data like a feeling of friendliness and produce warning signals like a sense of concern.

Now, in the case of the discarded metal, you do not know the history of the object. Unbeknownst to you, it happens to be a piece from a toy car that someone owned but lost a long time ago. At that time, the disc had accidentally gotten detached from the toy. The original owner is still searching for it. If you had met them, you would have probably handed them the disc because you would understand that it represents a precious memory in their life. Of course, you have no clue about this backstory. Still, as you are about to hurl the piece into the drain, a voice tells you to stop. It tells you to hold on to the metal because it might be important to someone. Now, this poses a conundrum in your mind. Should you adhere to your objective reality and throw the disc away? Should you follow your spirit and retain it? Ultimately, you listen to your inner voice. This case is an illustration of the true meaning of consciousness.

You received certain information from the environment via your non-sensory receptors. This information was relayed to you in the form of energy vibrations from the Universe that were emitted by the seeker of the toy. Your inner voice—the sixth sense—picked up these vibrations and conveyed them to you as a feeling of concern for others. The feeling was as real as the sensory information.

This is proof that consciousness is not just the awareness of the physical world; it is the awareness of both the objective and the spiritual worlds. The latter is the realm of perceptions, not sensations. It is a world of feelings, thoughts, and experiences. Like the material world, it is composed of energy. Unlike the material world, though, we do not know how to access it through the conventional methods of science, technology, or other types of materialistic pedagogy. The only known way of connecting with this world is through a range of practices that facilitate spiritual development.

How can we know for sure that the spiritual world exists?

Knowing is the wrong word. We *feel*. So, we *believe*. Thereafter, we *realize*.

From this enhanced definition of consciousness, we can conclude that a conscious person is aware of both their objective reality and the world that lies beyond it. There are four stages in the growth of a person's consciousness:

Asleep

This person is aware of their objective reality. They are conscious of their material needs, goals, and commitments.

They have dedicated their lives to accomplishing these objectives. However, they are unaware of the existence of the spiritual realm.

Aware

This person is well-informed about spiritual topics. They have gained this knowledge from the media and trusted people. However, they are not willing to make any sacrifices to embark on a journey of inner transformation.

Awake

This person is not only well-informed about spiritual topics, but they are also ready to embark on a journey of spiritual growth. To this end, they have worked on removing their barriers. They have made the necessary sacrifices. They have surrendered themselves and are devoted to a figure of their belief. From time to time, they have experienced a deep inner connection with the Universe. They are now on the way toward spiritual evolution.

Achiever

Remaining steadfast on their spiritual journey, this person has progressed. En route, they have developed many traits. They have continuously evolved and reinvented themselves. They exist in a permanent inner state of deep connectedness with the Universe.

Regardless of your state of conscious development, you can elevate spiritually by practicing preferred activities to attain a meditative state, resolving your barriers, surrendering to your beliefs, and making appropriate sacrifices. At the highest level of spiritual achievement, your consciousness will permanently merge with the ultimate consciousness—that of the Universe (*The One*). This supreme state of conscious development is known as the *State of Oneness*.

In this book, I have covered topics that are central to the growth of consciousness. Instead of exploring them in the form of essays, how-to guides, or lectures, I have presented them in a Q&A format. To make the answers accessible and relatable, I have combined philosophical explanations with stories. I hope this approach will provide you with the clarity and confidence to script your own spiritual journey.

Question 1

What Does It Mean to Be Awakened?

Around the world, millions of people lead a machine-like existence. They get up; consume their meals; go to school, college, or office; spend time with their families; watch TV; interact with mobile devices; and depart for the dreamland. This cycle is repeated day after day without any passion or enjoyment. Life is seen as a struggle to be endured, not a journey to be celebrated. Due to this view, most people sleepwalk through life—unmindful of the magical essence that flows through every living and nonliving being. They are alive, but not conscious; mobile, but not plugged in. Active, but not awakened.

Awakening is the realization that I am not alone and that I am part of a larger whole. This greater fabric of existence is the Universe itself. An awakened me is conscious of the energy that flows inside me and is aware that it is a constituent of the Universe.

In practical terms, what does it mean to be awake?

Let me share a personal example. Right now, I feel incredibly happy. My heart is bursting with so much love that I can feel it every millisecond. I cannot hold it any longer, so I must express it right now.

It began this morning. I woke up at 5:30 a.m. and walked to the neighboring park. To catch the early dawn, I sat down on an isolated bench to relax a bit and say hello to Nature. At best, I expected her to say "Hi" back. Instead, I received a gift that I could not have dreamt of in a million years—the gift of love. A warm hug, then a lingering sensuous kiss, followed by a deep, intimate conversation. Needless to say, the experience was unforgettable.

I could perceive everything. The chirping of birds as they flitted from one tree to another. The fresh scent of the plants and flowers. The dampness of the morning dew on my skin. I could hear every sound, feel every vibration, and smell each fragrance. I could see the tiniest ants going about their business. I was totally present in every moment. I felt conjoined with Mother Nature.

I was so conscious that I could feel Her pulse. I could understand what the birds were communicating. I could taste the fruits on the trees. I could see what the ants were building. Internally, I felt incredibly satisfied. There were no worries or anxieties clouding my mind. No fear of judgments, no fear of decisions. The only thing that mattered was *here* and *now*. I sat for half an hour, enjoying every moment of my newfound tranquillity. Will it be fleeting? Far from it!

Even after I had departed, the positive energy lingered within me. The whole day, I emitted it into my surroundings. My friends, colleagues, and even strangers flocked to me, drawn to its magnetism. "What is up with this guy? Is he taking something? How can he be so happy?" they must have wondered. In reality, I had not turned into a God-like happiness machine. I had experienced *Oneness*—a magical state of being wherein my soul had become synchronized with Nature, and I was radiating Her love back to my surroundings.

This is a snapshot of one day in my life. But the feeling, which I have described above, surges in me all the time.

Every day, I feel connected with everything and everyone, highly energized with positivity. I am fully aware of a higher power in the Universe because I can feel it pulsing within me. This is what makes me happy. This state of being is termed 'Awakening'. It is a mental and emotional condition wherein one is connected to the spirit of the Universe. A person in this state can perceive profound, universal truths and experience deep-rooted feelings. Let me recount an example to exemplify the awakening of a person.

In the epic, *Mahabharata*, Arjun, the warrior prince, is standing on the Kurukshetra battlefield. He is about to embark on a bloody war to win his kingdom back from his enemies. The antagonists happen to be the people he has known and loved his whole life. Faced with the horrifying prospect of killing them, he is filled with doubt. He tells his charioteer, Yogeshwar Krishna, that he wants to renounce the battle. The warrior's reluctance stems from his steadfast value system, with high principles—such as kinship, loyalty, and honor—its immutable elements. These values brought him into apparent conflict with his duty—to win the war for righteousness.

Tormented by these choices, Arjun asks Yogeshwar Krishna a vast array of questions that probe existential issues, such as the meaning of life. Instead of providing answers that conform to his beliefs, Yogeshwar Krishna challenges him by providing provocative, insightful answers. Through this interaction—documented in the *Bhagavad Gita*—Arjun gains the wisdom to acknowledge that there is a larger force that shapes us all and that we are destined to unite with it at some point. Life and death are just transitory phenomena taking place in this larger, permanent canvas. After ingesting these teachings, Arjun realizes that his sole duty is to lead his family's army into battle and to let go of the outcome. Consequently, he is able to detach himself from his value system—his most prized possession—while, at the same time, cherishing its tenets. Thereafter, he participates in the battle with gusto and reclaims the throne of Hastinapur from the Kauravas.

There is an Arjun in every one of us—a person bound by self-imposed barriers. In our daily lives, we feel like soldiers trying to survive a battle. So, we often adopt rules to guide and discipline us. By doing so, however, we straitjacket ourselves with restrictions that prevent us from connecting our consciousness to the Universe. Like Arjun, an awakened person can connect with the Universe by sensing the right thing to do. They can then perform their duty with aplomb without getting attached to its outcome.

You, too, can get awakened by being in the moment with Nature. This will help you to hone and refine your consciousness, and experience attachment with detachment. Like me, you will witness the magic of the Universe unfolding around you.

Question 2

What Is 'Being in the Moment'?

At every moment, each day, our mind is a running ticker tape of thoughts—both positive and negative—pertaining to the past and the future. These may be related to the things that we have done or that we plan to do. These may be related to the things that others have done or that they plan to do (at least in our minds!). These thoughts form a continuous wave of noise, like the static sound of an old CRT TV set—an item of nostalgia for those of us who have grown up watching television in the 80s.

This stream of thought gives rise to a constantly fluctuating current of emotions. Fear, anxiety, and depression at the negative end and satisfaction, connectedness, and peace at the positive end of the spectrum. These emotions continually get intense, then abate. Sometimes, they even morph into each other instantaneously. On the whole, we rarely feel emotionally stable due to the discomfort caused by this constant noise. So, we often express ourselves by being distracted, indifferent, impatient, or apathetic.

How does nature react to our unmindfulness?

Nature—like any living person—feeds off our attention and devotion. Like any conscious soul, she wants to express Her love to us and feel loved in return. So, when we are indifferent to Her expressions, abuse Her, or go against Her flow, she is unable to pass Her positive energy to us. Consequently, our latent positivity remains trapped and gets swamped by a swirl of negativity. On a daily basis, we feel like tired zombies—stuck in monotonous routines. We feel unappreciated, ignored, and unloved. A common symptom of this state of unconsciousness is the persistent feeling of drowsiness and fatigue that always pervades us, along with a sense of disappointment in the world for being unkind to us. These are all consequences of being out of sync with Nature's flow.

On the other hand, when we are in the moment, we feel alive. We may not have slept much the previous night. Perhaps less than four hours! Yet, we feel incredibly alert. This is because by being present in the moment, we are able to attune ourselves to the frequency of Nature. In this state of Oneness, we derive intense joy from even the minutest aspects of life—things that we deride, often ignore, for being inconsequential or stupid. In the state of Oneness, these mundane things assume cosmic significance.

That squirrel—whom we would never notice on our daily excursions—assumes the form of a messiah with a tail. Those pigeons—whom we would normally shoo away for littering our path—turn into minstrels crooning our good fortune. Those children in the playground—whom we would regard with annoyance and irritation—take on the form of playful wood fairies. Is it possible for anyone to feel negative in the presence of such delightful sights, sounds, and fragrances? Of course not! Here are a few examples of being present in the moment.

In the epic *Mahabharata,* Abhimanyu learns about a devastating battle formation called the *chakravyuha* (maze) from his father, Arjun, while he is in his mother's womb. Through the story, the unborn child imbibes the art of breaking into the maze but not how to escape from it. 17 years later, he faces the actual challenge of breaking into the chakravyuha and defeating a daunting adversary—the Kaurava army. Subsequently, Abhimanyu penetrates the maze and wages a valiant battle. However, he is killed in a manner that violates all the conventions and precepts of warfare.

At the same time, Yogeshwar Krishna—his uncle and father's guide—accompanies Arjun to a different war front set up by the Kauravas for diversionary purposes. He is well aware of Abhimanyu's trap. Yet, he is not overwhelmed by fear or anxiety. He neither informs Arjun of his son's precarious situation nor does he rush to his aid. He chooses to be in the moment, as a witness, and let things run their natural course. In other words, he decides not to interfere in the workings of fate. Consequently, Abhimanyu succumbs to the battle.

Was there a larger purpose to Yogeshwar Krishna's decision? Yes. He could see that *adharma* (unrighteousness) had taken root in the land. To reestablish righteousness, the enemy's deceptive and manipulative tactics had to be turned against them. However, at that stage of the battle, Arjun and the Pandavas were far too encumbered by the principles of virtue to wage an effective war. Thus, Abhimanyu's death was a necessary sacrifice to accomplish a larger goal—the restoration of *dharma*.

Another example of a person who was always present in the moment is the revolutionary Bhagat Singh. He was scheduled to be executed on March 23, 1931. In the days leading to his death, he spent much of his time reading Lenin's biography. In fact, he was so engrossed in the ideas of a fellow revolutionary and kindred spirit that the dark clouds of doom did not loom on his mental horizon. What appeared in their place? The resplendent rays of hope and self-belief! On the day of his execution, the warden asked him to pray to *Wahe Guru* (God). Bhagat Singh was in such positive spirits that he laughed at this directive. He said that he had never prayed in his life. By doing so at this juncture, he would look like a coward before the Lord.

From these stories, it is evident that by being present in the moment, we can remain attached to everything while staying detached. Therefore, we can experience the incredible pleasure of becoming intimately connected with the Universe. At the same time, we would not be influenced by the result. In this state of being—that of a passionate witness—we can experience fulfillment in all situations, favorable and adverse.

The only feeling that courses through our veins when we are present in the moment is satisfaction. A deep, lasting sense of satisfaction. This is a feeling that is neither halting or static like the white noise that afflicts us on a daily basis, nor a feeling that dies prematurely in our souls. This feeling is lasting because we emit it to others and to the environment. As a result, we make the Universe happier. This is the true definition of happiness. It is not what we feel, but what we radiate. Our contribution to the universal bounty of positive energy.

Thus, to experience happiness, you do not have to necessarily embark on a world-changing endeavor. All you have to do is be present in the moment by being attentive to Nature. She will reciprocate with more love than you could ever imagine.

Question 3

What Is the State of 'Ultimate Consciousness'?

Have you ever been in a state of existence wherein you were intimately connected with your surroundings? Could you perceive the activities of Nature at an atomic level, even the thoughts of people? Did you experience a tingling sensation running through your that made you feel alive? Was your mind so clear of the cobwebs of doubt that you could clearly identify the right decision to make? Was your heart bursting with so much love that you just had to express it? If you answered "Yes" to all these questions, then you have experienced the state of Oneness.

Oneness is a state of supreme consciousness in which a person is connected with the origin of the Universe, i.e., *The One*. It is the source of all energy that shapes every living and nonliving being in the cosmos. In this state of being, a person experiences the following:

1. Perfect synchronization with Nature
2. Presence in every moment as a witness
3. Tremendous love for all beings, while remaining detached
4. Harmonious energy flow in sync with Nature
5. Awareness of all things
6. Perpetual satisfaction
7. Happiness that radiates perpetually energizing others

To achieve the state of Oneness, we need to go through a process of inner filtration to remove our barriers or inhibitions. We can then attain a deep meditative state and connect with The One with the help of different routines, for e.g., the pursuit of passions, daily activities of life, meditation practices, etc. Once we are connected, it is possible for us to remain in this state for as long as we want and experience deep and lasting fulfillment. Here are a few examples of individuals who attained this supremely conscious state of being.

Buddha achieved Oneness by following the path of nonviolence and engaging in deep meditation. Jagat Guru Shankaracharya (700–750 AD), on the other hand, reestablished *Sanatan Dharma* in the wake of the dominant faith of his time, Buddhism. A spiritual seeker, he left home at the age of eight and traveled across India, engaging in discussions with the leading minds of the day, crafting path breaking literary works, and setting up several influential spiritual communes. Through the pursuit of philosophy, he was able to attain the state of Oneness.

In this context, we must also pay homage to the towering figures of western religions. Jesus Christ reached the state of supreme consciousness through sacrifice and selfless service. Moses achieved the same by exhibiting courage in the face of tremendous adversity. Through the sheer power of belief, the Prince of Egypt single-handedly took on the forces of Pharaoh Rameses and defeated them.

The stories of these individuals have been well documented by scholars throughout history. They may have lived in different eras, thrived in different cultures, and followed different paths, but all of them reached the same destination—the state of Oneness—where their consciousness merged with the origin of the Universe.

Question 4

How Does One Connect with 'The Ultimate'?

Today, I connected with the origin of the Universe, *Yog*. Many people call this 'God'. Others have named it 'The Almighty'. Quite a few refer to it as 'The Higher Power'. For the sake of neutrality, I will refer to this essence of life as 'The One'.

My mode of connecting with The One is through deep meditation practices. I have learned many techniques in the course of my life. These techniques have been instrumental in helping me synchronize my thoughts and feelings with Nature. However, there are other ways to achieve a deep spiritual connection. The pursuit of passions offers one such pathway.

An author may forge a connection by writing about their pain; a musician, by composing a piece that celebrates a glorious event; a social worker, by feeding hungry children; and a mother, by teaching her child to swim. There are infinite ways to achieve this cosmic connection and to reach the state of Oneness. The only common requirement for completing this journey is having an open, non judgmental mentality and devotion to a figure (a person, object, idea, etc.) of belief. Here are some examples of people who were able to connect with the origin of the Universe through the pursuit of their passions.

Sachin Tendulkar is often referred to, by the sobriquet, as the 'God of Cricket'. While his incredible accomplishments definitely validate this nickname, his serene, monk-like approach toward batting is another crucial contributor to it. When Sachin takes guard, he feels himself blending with the world. At that point in time, the opposition becomes irrelevant. Anger, fear, and other negative emotions melt away. The only thing that matters to him is that moment, and he experiences complete bliss.

Similarly, Michael Jackson and Bruce Lee were able to reach this state of being through their passions—dance and martial arts, respectively.

Apart from the pursuit of passions, it is also possible to achieve this state through daily activities or routines in one's life. Guru Ravidas (1450–1520), the founder of the Ravidassia religion, was a mystic poet and *sant* from Varanasi. He was the Guru of Ma Meera—the legendary poet and devotee of Yogeshwar Krishna. Guru Ravidas was a cobbler who attained the highest level of consciousness through the diligent practice of his professional routine—leathercraft.

Once we harness the power of this Onesome connection, it is possible to banish all our preconceived judgments and become completely neutral. In this state, I feel attached to everything and everyone but detached at the same time. I remain in the role of a passionate witness throughout my meditative journey. Every moment comes alive, and I feel deeply satisfied at every instant. Throughout the day and the next, I radiate my positive energy to others, bringing smiles to their faces and comfort in their hearts.

Whether you believe in Higher Power or not, one fact is indisputable: there exists a force that runs through all beings, shaping and evolving them over time. This is *The One*. It does not judge right or wrong, good or bad. It simply lets us do our own thing and allows matters to follow their natural course. We can connect with The One through celebration. We can even connect with it through pain. The point is that when we are connected with this force through the power of our belief, we feel satisfied and emit positivity, and conversely, if we are not, we feel dissatisfied and transmit our negativity onto others.

What is your road to Oneness?

Question 5

Is Devotion Necessary?

Oneness is a state of existence wherein a person is connected with The One, i.e., the source of the Universe's energy. The process of connection is individual specific. We can immerse ourselves in a specific process and undertake a journey of spiritual growth to eventually connect with The One, or we may choose a process depending on our nature, talent, and preference. Irrespective of the path that we choose, devotion to the *Guru Tatwa* is the key requirement for forging a deep connection.

The Guru Tatwa, i.e., the element of the Guru, is the supreme consciousness that one seeks to attain. It is super-energy that manifests itself in different forms. We may feel this energy within a person, a plant, an animal, or even an inanimate object like a book. The embodiment of this spirit is the Guru. Irrespective of the manifestation, our affection for our Guru should be unconditional, i.e., we love our Guru without expecting anything in return.

It is through our devotion to the Guru Tatwa that we can cast aside our ego and accept the supremacy of Nature. Only then, are we able to free our minds from preconceived judgments and experience child like awe, wonderment, and innocence. In this state of being, we flow with the energy of the Universe and enjoy deep satisfaction. Here is an example of an individual's devotion to their Guru Tatwa.

The *Bhagavata Purana* contains a story about a demon, Prahlad, and his devotion to Lord Vishnu. Prahlad's father, Hiranyakashipu, was an extremely evil titan king with the boon of near immortality. He was upset with his son's devotion to Lord Vishnu—a spiritual inclination that he had inculcated by listening to the chants of Narada, the divine sage, in his mother's womb. After numerous failed attempts at persuading his son to change his faith, the demon potentate could not take it anymore and decided to kill Prahlad.

Hiranyakashipu then made repeated attempts to murder his son. He tried to poison him, dropped him in a snake pit, and even tried to get him trampled by elephants. However, on every occasion, the boy scripted a miraculous escape— owing to his devotion to Lord Vishnu. Notwithstanding these failures, Hiranyakashipu did not stop. He kept trying to kill the boy. Each time, he came closer to the result, but somehow, his efforts were always thwarted.

Finally, when all seemed lost for Prahlad, the boy surrendered himself to the deity. He invoked Lord Vishnu to manifest himself from a stone pillar. Lord Vishnu then appeared in the form of Narasimha—half-man, half-lion. The chimaera lifted Hiranyakashipu with its mighty arms, placed him on its thighs, and ripped him to shreds with its ferocious claws.

This example is a great illustration of the power of devotion. It shows us that devotion and belief can help us accomplish incredible feats—acts we would never have thought possible.

However, devotion cannot be forced. It must come from within. We must first surrender to the Guru by making sacrifices to remove our inhibitions. Sacrifice kindles the flame of love for the Guru Tatwa, thereby accelerating our journey to a deeper state of consciousness. Thereafter, we develop the faith to fully surrender ourselves to the Guru. Upon surrendering, we experience a surge of love. A surge that connects us deeper with The One and makes us radiate happiness, energizing the Universe.

Question 6

Do We Need to Surrender?

If commitment is a leopard, sacrifice is a saber-toothed tiger—a beast that exists in myth, not in real life. Notwithstanding our belief, it is undeniable that the beast of sacrifice will cross our path at certain stages in life. While avoidance ensures survival, engagement helps us evolve.

Sacrifice is a test thrown at us by Nature to filter out our inner negativity and to help us become open, positive, and non judgmental. In this state of being, we can dig deeper to expand our consciousness and radiate more positive energy. Sacrifice involves the forsaking of guaranteed rewards or benefits to unlock our barriers and, eventually, merge with The One.

During the course of our lives, we face numerous situations where we have to make a sacrifice. The objective of the sacrifice often appears to be short term. However, they do satisfy our long-term objective of achieving conscious growth. Sacrifice involves taking a risk or a leap of faith. It may or may not produce the result that we had expected. Irrespective of the outcome, the learnings from sacrifice and self-awareness propel us to a higher level of consciousness. Thereafter, we face different, possibly more complex, choices. These choices require us to make further sacrifices but propel us to reach a higher level of consciousness.

An example of sacrifice in daily life is that of a person who must make a sizeable financial investment to launch a new company. Here, they have to sacrifice financial security to become a successful entrepreneur. Subsequently, when they have to raise external growth capital, they have to dilute their stake to an investor. Evidently, they must sacrifice ownership and control to achieve their long-term business goals.

The importance of sacrifice is illustrated in the epic *Ramayana*. Would Shri Ram have attained enlightenment had he not sacrificed his throne and gone into exile? Therefore, to grow our consciousness, we must make sacrifices that come our way instead of avoiding them like scared cats.

While sacrifice is crucial for conscious growth, it is not sufficient to achieve Oneness. As mentioned before, to attain the ultimate state of super consciousness, we must surrender to the Guru Tatwa (the element of supreme consciousness). Surrendering ourselves to it represents the ultimate form of sacrifice. It involves total submission to a figure of our belief—an entity (living or nonliving) that, we feel, is lustrous in the energy of The One. To kindle this energy, we must sacrifice our ultimate possession—our belief—to the Guru Tatwa. When we do that, we bank 100% on the belief that our Guru Tatwa will guide and strengthen us in all scenarios. Our belief factor activates the energy, which then awakens our consciousness. Here are three examples of the growth of consciousness following one's surrender to the Guru Tatwa.

The first example is the story of an archer, Ekalavya, as depicted in the *Mahabharata*. Ekalavya was an aspiring warrior who dreamed of training under Dronacharaya, the legendary military instructor from a rival kingdom. Ekalavya expressed his devotion to Guru Drona through a nonliving symbol of his consciousness. Awakened by its energy, he believed that

Guru Drona would help and guide him in his ambition. The power of his belief made him the finest archer in his land.

Another example of surrender can be found in the tale of Draupadi, chronicled in the *Mahabharata*. Draupadi was the wife of the five accomplished Pandava brothers. She was widely regarded as the most beautiful, sought-after, and respected woman in the world. However, her eldest husband, Yudhishthira, lost her in a game of chance to his cousin, Duryodhana, of the Kaurava clan. Following that defeat, she was subjected to public humiliation by the Kauravas, while her powerful husbands could only look on helplessly. In full view of the attendees of the Royal Court of Hastinapur, Dushasana tried to disrobe her. However, Draupadi surrendered herself to Yogeshwar Krishna and prayed to him for protection. To the surprise of Dushasana and everyone else, her sari turned into an endless river of fabric. As a result, she could not be disrobed, and her honor remained intact. Her surrender to Yogeshwar Krishna was so pure and complete that she was saved from harm.

The life story of Swami Vivekananda (1863–1902), a monk from Kolkata, is another illustration of surrendering to one's Guru Tatwa. The Swami was a disciple of the mystic Thakur Ramkrishna. After becoming his adherent, Vivekananda surrendered himself completely to his Guru. His devotion was so pure and intense that at the Parliament of World Religions in Chicago (1893), attendees and participants could feel the energy of Thakur Ramkrishna emanating from Swami and pervading the august halls of the venue. Thereafter, he became the voice of his Guru and carried his message to millions of people around the world by writing books and setting up a spiritual order for social service called the *Ramakrishna Mission*.

These stories are significant because they show that true greatness lies not in the disciple nor the master, but in the belief in one's Guru. Similarly, we too have the divine flame within us. All we need to kindle it are two things: belief in something or someone and faith in our belief.

Question 7

Are We All Connected?

When I was a primary school student, my science teacher taught us that atoms are the building blocks of all objects.

'These teeny tiny materials combine with each other to constitute everything in the Universe,' he said.

In college, I was presented with a more granular view of matter. There are particles that are way tinier than atoms. This discovery made me wonder, *What is the fundamental constituent of the Universe? What is it that cannot be created nor destroyed?* The answer is energy.

Energy is the force that makes up everything in the Universe—tangible and intangible. You and I are made of energy. Ditto for our thoughts and feelings. Based on this proposition, we can conclude that everything and everyone in the Universe is connected. It is the loop that binds us all—an infinite, cosmic energy chain. This connection can be perceived in the form of an aura of energy composition, radiating outward from every being.

The ocean's surface is a good illustration of this phenomenon. Its color appears to be green due to changes in the wavelength of light as it travels through the body of water. This occurrence is known as 'The Raman Effect'.

Like the ocean's color, the aura of every being may alter due to changes in circumstances, moods, or inner satisfaction levels. So, when we feel anxious, frustrated, or sad, our energy feels damp and mellow to others. This repels people from interacting with us. Even a nonliving object, like a book, toy, or painting, emits an aura that is influenced by events that are involved with it. Depending on its constitution, the aura can affect the well-being of anyone interacting with it, either positively or adversely. To understand this phenomenon better, here is an example of the energy composition theory:

During the crisis of the Mahishasura War, the deities—Vishnu, Shiva, Brahma, and many others—pooled their collective energy resources (*shakti*) to create a deity, Ma Durga. Endowed with their combined energy, this entity was able to vanquish the fearsome and formidable enemy, Mahishasura.

This example shows that even though everything that is external appears to be separate from us—it is not. We are all different manifestations of the same energy that shapes the Universe. We are not disparate bodies, destined to live in isolation. We intertwine as flowing energies, interconnected and bound. Our common purpose? To reunite at our origin.

For anything in the world to flow, be it a river, a cloud of steam, or a person, its constituents must be in sync. Thus, a river becomes an ocean only when every drop flows harmoniously into the massive water body. Similarly, the population of the world is a flow that, itself, is a part of the larger movement of energy in the Universe. Like the river, the human species evolves when it is in harmony with its 'ocean'—the Universe. This can happen only when every 'droplet', i.e., human being, is in sync with the Universe.

How do we go out of sync with the Universe?

When we are born, we are like saplings. Our hearts are open, our minds fluid. We are devoid of judgment and preconceptions. At this stage of life, we allow every bit of information from the world to seep into our souls, unfiltered, ensuring that we are in a state of perfect flow. This is when our consciousness is most fertile. However, as we get older, we get clouded by the 'noise' that emanates from our environment—opinions, biases, etc. This information cloud makes us judgmental, preventing us from inviting the world in. In adulthood, the 'noise' is a storm of information that brings confusion and fear in its wake.

We are all familiar with the symptoms of the noise. Anxieties, worries, doubts, stresses, fears, and so many other types of negativity. As a result, we foment negative energy in our surroundings and lose our balance. Consequently, we are not able to enjoy the moment. This is extremely detrimental to our levels of life satisfaction.

Life is a collection of moments, and life satisfaction is the cumulative enjoyment of every moment. Thus, the key to being happy is to always be in the moment, cherishing and loving every creation of the Universe.

Question 8

Do We Have to
Renounce Everything?

It is commonly believed that after fulfilling one's social and family responsibilities, achieving one's life goals, and satisfying one's material and emotional needs, a person must forsake all worldly pleasures. This view is a key tenet of Sanatan philosophy, although it exists in a more subdued form in the Abrahamic family of religions. The age-old idea of renunciation is premised on the belief that it will help an individual experience greater happiness, peace, enlightenment, or salvation.

In all religions, renunciation is an essential aspect of spiritual growth. In Sanatan philosophy, *sanyas* is a stage of life that one must go through—a stage where a person must renounce all material attachments, distance themselves from their family and friends, and head off to a secluded place.

Is sanyas necessary for achieving conscious growth?

To expand one's consciousness, a person must be connected with The One. This can happen only if the individual is fully in the moment, enjoying every instant. To undergo such an experience, we have to passionately witness our surroundings—observing, enjoying, and being involved with them but being detached nonetheless.

An example of this hyper-conscious, neutral state of being is the spectatorship of a match. The spectators clap, cheer, eat dozens of hot dogs, pass comments, and hug neighbors, but they never participate in the actual game. They simply relish their outing. They are able to move on emotionally, even if the outcome is not to their liking. Thus, a passionate witness is someone who is attached to the game while remaining detached. They can enjoy every moment to its fullest and emit positivity continuously.

On the other hand, the abjurer of the sport experiences a swollen ego on account of their actions. This is because they are so attached to the righteousness of their actions that they become judgmental of contrarian views. Consequently, they harbor negativity and lose their inner balance—paradoxically, the very quality that they strove to strengthen. Thus, there is no need to renounce the sport because it is possible to emit happiness by enjoying its aspects while remaining unattached to its outcome. In other words, sanyas is a state of being, not an act or a phase. Here are two examples of people who spent their lives in this state.

Raja Janaka, the father of Sita, was the ruler of the ancient kingdom of Videha in the Mithila region. He was known as the philosophical king who was detached from all worldly pleasures. Raja Janaka had an avid interest in spiritual discourse and engaged in numerous discussions and interactions with sages from all corners of the country. The revered seeker, Ashtavakra, became his Guru. Although the king was deeply spiritual, he did not abandon his world to sequester himself in a remote region. He actively ruled his kingdom and performed all his duties with aplomb. Yet, he maintained an attitude of detachment throughout his life.

Guru Gobind Singh (1666–1708), the tenth Sikh Guru, was a warrior, poet, and spiritual master. He established the *Guru Parampara* by finalizing the Guru Granth Sahib, the primary scripture of Sikhism. His detachment from everything was tested by the Mughal governor of Sirhind, Wazir Khan. The administrator had captured Guru Gobind Singh's two youngest sons, aged 5 and 8, respectively. He then threatened to execute them unless the Guru converted to Islam. However, Guru Gobind Singh's principle of detachment and his conviction in his values enabled him to resist the Mughal leader's threats. Even though his sons were eventually murdered, the Guru refused to convert to Islam.

Contrary to the media hype that is often lavished on those who abandon their worlds for a supposedly higher spiritual cause, these examples of renunciation prove that we do not have to forsake our attachments and move to an isolated place to pursue conscious growth. We may remain where we are, fulfilling our existing commitments, fully in the moment while detached from the outcomes.

If we apply the lessons to various spheres of life, we realize that we can be in the following state at all times:

> *One foot in the ocean, the other on the beach.*
> *One on the mountain, the other in the valley.*
> *One on the forest green, the other up high.*

In the state of Oneness—illustrated above—we become the Universe's candlesticks for kindling its energy. Renunciation is, therefore, unnecessary because it would only deprive us of the wax for molding our consciousness.

Question 9

How Can We Free Our Minds from Judgments?

S ince the time we gain awareness, we are constantly bombarded with information. Most of this consists of news and facts about the world. However, a significant portion of this information is comprised of the opinions and views of people. All this forms a cloud of noise in our minds, compelling us to issue judgments and conclusions.

Judgment is the expression of our assumptions that are based on information we gather from the environment. Over time, these assumptions constitute a belief system that forms the bedrock of our identity. Thereafter, we find it hard to look beyond these assumptions, even when situations arise where we would benefit from being mentally flexible. In those situations, we feel outraged by the attack on our prized assumptions. Our ego gets hurt. Consequently, we are filled with negative thoughts, and we exude these sentiments into our environment, upsetting our energy balance with the Universe. Individuals who attain a state of mind that is empty of judgment (*Vicharo ki Shunyata*) are able to disregard conventional wisdom and take decisions while remaining fully present in the moment. In doing so, they are primed to achieve ultimate consciousness. Here are a few examples.

Mahendra Singh Dhoni, the former captain of the Indian cricket team, has achieved a judgment-free mental disposition. His mindset was evident during the final match of the World T20 Cup between India and Pakistan in 2007. In the final over of the match, Pakistan needed to score 13 runs to secure victory. Most leaders would have turned to their experienced performers at that juncture. In fact, the spin bowling stalwart, Harbhajan Singh, had another over to go. However, Dhoni did not rely on his thespian. He turned to the unheralded and inexperienced Joginder Singh to bowl the final over. That decision proved to be a masterstroke. Joginder contained the marauding Pakistani batsmen to just 8 runs and secured a famous victory.

In the world of science, Albert Einstein is a great exemplar of this state of mind. He displayed a remarkable capacity for suspending judgment. This allowed him to critically analyze even the most established scientific principles of his time. While Newtonian physics represented entrenched dogma within the scientific community, Einstein maintained an open and inquisitive mind and was unwilling to accept any 'Gospel Truths' without rigorous questioning. Through disciplined contemplation unfettered by preconceptions, he identified limitations in the prevailing models of motion and gravitation. This judgment-free framework empowered Einstein to conceive his groundbreaking theory of relativity, founded on fresh paradigms that challenged centuries of conventional wisdom. Rather than dismissing dissenting ideas out of hand, Einstein approached them with impartial consideration and courageously pursued his original theories even when they contravened dominant thought. It was this disciplined lack of bias that equipped Einstein to revolutionize physics and overturn classical mechanics through revolutionary new frameworks founded solely on logic and evidence over established prestige.

On the other hand, Mahatma Gandhi's enormous political and social successes can be attributed, in large part, to his remarkable ability to consider opposing viewpoints without immediate judgment or condemnation. In an era when violence and rebellion were widely accepted as the only means for change, Gandhi maintained an open mind and did not take conventional ideologies as benchmarks for any actions. Through calm analysis unfettered by preconceptions, he developed the philosophy of *ahimsa*, or nonviolence—a revolutionary concept at the time.

Armed with ahimsa and a judgment-free willingness to understand all perspectives, Gandhi skilfully launched campaigns like the Non-Cooperation Movement that attracted widespread, cross-sectional support.

His nonjudgmental approach permitted constructive engagement even with colonial British rule, facilitating positive change through consensus instead of conflict. He remained unwavering in the espousal of his principles, despite facing tremendous pressure from his followers to compromise at times.

On February 4, 1922, a violent incident occurred in Chauri Chaura, located in modern-day Uttar Pradesh, where a police station was set ablaze by a crowd of protesters affiliated with the Independence Movement, resulting in the deaths of 22 British India army officers. Appalled by the flagrant contravention of ahimsa, Mahatma Gandhi halted the Non-Cooperation movement a week later.

In essence, Gandhi's refusal to judge others and his open-minded pursuit of truth above established norms empowered formidable political initiatives that ultimately led to India's independence through nonviolent civil disobedience.

In the same context, the epic *Ramayana* tells us the tale of Bali and his brother, Sugriva. Bali, the king of Kishkindha, was immensely powerful and had built a reputation as a formidable warrior. He had even defeated Ravana, the demonic ruler and captor of Sita, the wife of Shri Ram. Conventional wisdom dictated that Shri Ram seek the help of Bali to rescue his wife. On the contrary, he turned to Sugriva—the far less-experienced fighter—because he was disturbed by Bali's vengeful expulsion of his brother from Kishkindha.

In *Mahabharata*, both Arjun and his mortal enemy, Duryodhana, sought the help of Yogeshwar Krishna to win the Battle of Kurukshetra. Yogeshwar Krishna offered the feuding brothers two options. They could take his army— the mighty legion of Dwarka—or himself sans weapons and powers. While Duryodhana gleefully selected the army, Arjun realized that the ultimate consciousness was the most potent weapon at his disposal. Thus, he filtered out the accepted battle logic—strength lies in numbers and machinery—and chose Yogeshwar Krishna as his charioteer and guide.

These examples demonstrate that it is important to empty ourselves of judgments in order to stay connected with The One. In such a state, negative thoughts and feelings would disappear, and we would feel fully present in the moment. In order to reach this state, we must be open to suspending our assumptions and emptying our minds, like a vessel, of all judgments.

How can we empty ourselves of judgment?

I have tried a meditation exercise called 'Gibberish'. To perform this activity, I speak aloud in a language that is completely alien to me. I persist with this activity for 5–10 minutes. After that my mind feels considerably lighter. Another meditation technique that works well is *Maun* (Silence). For about 4–6 hours, I remain in my room. I do not communicate with anyone via any mode. Thereafter, my heart feels more open and welcoming to others.

Information is said to be the source of power. However, it can also be a source of agony and negativity as well. Remove the fungus of judgment from your consciousness and attain a happier, more conscious state of being.

Question 10

What Is The Purpose of Life?

*W*ho am I? Why am I here? What do I want to do with my life?

If you are looking for answers to these questions, you are searching for a purpose in your life. These questions surface at different stages, irrespective of one's state of satisfaction, although they are more pervasive during periods of darkness and dissatisfaction.

Purpose refers to the reason for one's existence. In modern society, this term is commonly understood as a goal that has to be chased. According to this interpretation of the word, the life goal or objective is a prize. It can be a tangible object, i.e., money or material things. Alternatively, it can be something intangible, like fame or appreciation. Notwithstanding its form, many people believe that they will find happiness once they achieve this prize. The real experience, however, is starkly different from that depicted in the media and popular culture. Here is a case study of a person who views purpose as a goal.

A mountaineer set different goals at various points in his life. These included the conquest of peaks from Kilimanjaro to Everest. He was focused on these targets because he was eyeing the rewards at the end of each excursion. Let us assume that he was successful in achieving each target. Obviously, he felt satisfied after every victory. But then, expectations were foisted on him by the overzealous public. Trying to meet those expectations, he became anxious and stressed. Thus, his experience of chasing purpose as a goal led to negative emotions, not happiness. However, if he interpreted purpose as a calling, his experience could have been radically different.

If you asked the mountaineer, "Why did you take up the sport?" he would introspect and tell you that the mountain called his name. It was a call that he had to heed. This is because he wanted to connect with The One and mountaineering was the medium his consciousness chose to establish this link. Through this activity, he could reach a state of divine connectedness, wherein he could become one with the Universe. Once he entered this zone, he became a happiness dynamo, absorbing and radiating positive energy. External rewards did not matter to him. He was happy simply because he was connected to Nature.

Thus, the purpose of life is to expand our consciousness until it aligns with the One. We can all get there by following our calling, thereby becoming superconscious. Here are two examples of people who discovered the purpose of life.

Siddhartha was born in Lumbini (modern-day Nepal) to an aristocratic family. He became disillusioned with the materialism of his three-dimensional world and chose to renounce it at the age of 30. Galvanized by the need to achieve higher consciousness, he became a monk. Five years later, he attained supreme consciousness and came to be known as the Buddha. Thereafter, he developed the 'Eight-Fold Path'—a balanced approach to conscious development that straddled the extremes of self-indulgence and asceticism. This middle way became the cornerstone of the philosophy of Buddhism and its global acceptance.

Ashoka the Great—Emperor of the Mauryan dynasty—ruled the Indian sub-continent from 268–232 BC. His tenure can be divided into two parts—pre and post-Kalinga. In the first segment of his rule, he was enamored by worldly pleasures and had a proclivity for violence. The use of force became his calling card during the Kalinga War in 260 BC. This brutal battle resulted in the deaths of 100,000 people, although it cemented Ashoka's preeminence in the global imperial order. After the victory, he was filled with regret. He deplored the violent and inhumane methods that he had deployed to annex the kingdom. Subsequently, he was compelled to seek penance and attain higher consciousness by converting to Buddhism. Thereafter, a new chapter in his leadership began that was marked by the institution of several Buddhist councils and the propagation of Buddhist teachings around the world.

These examples illustrate that the purpose of life is not the quest for power, glory, or otherworldly attainments. It is a pursuit of the growth of consciousness. When we reach a state of consciousness, we are in the moment with Nature—observing and feeling every sight, sound, and fragrance with passionate detachment.

Imagine if we could remain in this state permanently; we would flow for eternity!

Question 11

How Can We
Experience Love?

Most of us seek love, yearning for its presence from friends and family, colleagues, and even strangers. Our understanding of love is limited to some acts: expressions of appreciation, intimacy, kindness, connection, or anything that makes us feel special. In our minds, these acts must be reciprocal in order to be binding. However, real-world experiences suggest that bonds formed on the basis of these acts are fleeting. The tendency to associate love with conditional affection is misguided as the true essence of love is far more sweeping and magical.

Love is an inner state of unbridled devotion to the Universe. When we are in this state, we experience an irresistible desire to merge with The One. As this sensation floods our being, we feel compelled to share it with everybody and everything, irrespective of our prior association with that person, creature, or object. In the state of love, we express our feelings for all beings with equal intensity.

We show affection to both our companion and to a water bottle with equal fervor. We hold our friend's hands and a stranger's with a similar passion. We cuddle our baby and a baby elephant with even affection. Thus, love transcends all barriers of race, species, time, geography, etc. Love is pure, eternal, and universal. Here is an example of the purity of love.

Ma Meera was a mystic poet and saint from Rajasthan who lived in the sixteenth century. She was born in a royal family. Intensely spiritual from birth, she became an ardent devotee of Yogeshwar Krishna. Her love for the God of Tenderness knew no bounds. She even sacrificed her wealth and social status so that she could devote her life to him. Ma Meera expressed her feelings for Yogeshwar Krishna through songs and poems. Since her death, the hymns have become the bulwark of devotional music in India. It is said that when she died, her energy fused with that of her beloved Yogeshwar Krishna idol, and her body disappeared.

The philosophy of Oneness provides an explanation for this apparently miraculous phenomenon. Ma Meera's love for Yogeshwar Krishna was so deep that when she died, her energy fused with her Guru Tatwa, melding the two into a composite entity that merged with The One.

Apart from being pure, love is also enduring and universal. This means that it is not restricted to three-dimensional exchanges between physical bodies. It does not stop where life, space, or time end. Here is an example that demonstrates the timelessness of love.

In the movie *Interstellar* (2014), an astronaut named Cooper abandons his daughter, Murphy, for a space mission to save humanity from extinction. He gets lost in a black hole in the distant future—an ethereal place from where he sees her life unfold. Cooper knows that he is already dead in his daughter's world and that it is practically impossible for him to see her again. Even if he were to return to Earth, she would probably be dead. However, his love for her is so strong that his heart brims with hope. So, he sends her messages in Morse code from the black hole. These messages contain data on how to build an escape shuttle. At the same time, Murphy's love for her father burns in secret within her, compelling her to believe that he will return someday. Her belief factor enables her to discard conventional scientific logic, accept the other-dimensional messages, and decode the formula therein to build the spacecraft. Eventually, Cooper is ejected from the black hole. He returns to the Earth of the future, where he is reunited with Murphy—an old lady now.

Therefore, love is transcendental and extends beyond action, space, and time. It is far more sweeping than selective acts of endearment for favored individuals, e.g., the purchase of flowers for a companion. It is a state of being where we radiate positive feelings for all beings, without discrimination.

What do you have to do to experience love?

Be in the moment and feel the vibrations of the Universe. You will feel as if you are in the midst of an eternal embrace.

Question 12

How Can We Experience Attachment With Detachment?

During the course of our lives, we make numerous decisions and perform many actions to fulfil our desires and commitments. We exercise our belief system by pronouncing various judgments on issues, people, and objects. Consequently, we get attached to the foci of our judgments about individuals, things, and even the beliefs themselves. Over time, these attachments trap us in a cycle of *karma*, wherein we are forced to pay our dues as the consequences of our thoughts and deeds over many life cycles. As a result, negative thoughts and feelings assail us at various times, disturbing our inner peace and stymying our life satisfaction levels.

The path to evolving consciousness to the state of Oneness requires one to transcend attachments. In this supreme state of being, all judgments evaporate, thereby, emptying the soul.

Does this mean that we have to necessarily eliminate all attachments? No. Because if that were so, the only route for the pursuit of conscious growth would have been renunciation. However, we know that the mere renunciation of worldly pleasures and the retreat to seclusion does not guarantee the conscious growth of an individual. *Why?*

It is very likely that the renouncer would remain attached to the values associated with their newfound calling. Their enhanced belief system would then enflame their ego. It would compel them to harbor thoughts and perform actions that would ensnare them in the karmic cycle, instead of liberating them. Thus, the removal of all attachments is not necessary for achieving supreme consciousness. On the other hand, being attached is not the way forward either.

What is the ideal state for achieving supreme consciousness?

The ideal state for conscious development is *attachment with detachment*. When a person exists in this condition, they can choose to attach themselves to something, while remaining detached at the same time. A simple example to illustrate this concept is that of an audience member viewing a panel discussion. At this event, the witness feels excited by the topic, conversations, and mannerisms of the speakers. They are anonymous, yet their existence is noted. Moreover, they are liberated from the actual act of participation—an act that would lead to their attachment with the outcome and their inevitable bondage in the karmic cycle.

Maharshi Dadhichi personifies the state of attachment with detachment. When Indra, the king of the Devas, was driven out of Devalok by the serpent king, Vritra, he turned to Vishnu for guidance. The Preserver of the Universe informed him that the only weapons that could kill the demonic enemy would have to be forged from the thunder-imbued bones of the sage, Maharshi Dadhichi. Indra approached Maharshi Dadhichi and asked him to spare his body for the conflict. Maharshi Dadhichi had already achieved a supreme level of consciousness. He was always present in the moment and deeply connected with the origin of the Universe. The prospect of death did not scare him. He agreed to donate his body to

Devas' cause. Subsequently, a large collection of weapons was fashioned out of his bones. The most famous one was a thunderbolt. Indra wielded it to potent effect and killed Vritra.

Another example of an individual who has attained this state is that of, as mentioned earlier, Mahendra Singh Dhoni, the former captain of the Indian cricket team. When a great athlete is in the twilight of his career, we often see them getting attached to the records. They are constantly thinking of setting benchmarks that will never be crossed. They are obsessed with enshrining their name in the history books for all time to come. This attachment with records is the primary driver for legends to perform beyond their expiration dates.

However, M.S. Dhoni is an exception to the legend chasers. When he played his 99th test match, there were few calls for retirement from selectors and the public alike. He could have gone on and on like many sportsmen in the past. He could have played 100 tests, maybe even more, with diminishing returns. He did not. Dhoni loved the sport of cricket and realized that his impact could extend far beyond the roles of captain, wicketkeeper, and batsman. He was not attached to records for his own sake. His retirement before his 100th test is a wonderful example of a person who has attained attachment with detachment in our time.

How can one practically attain this state?

While the attainment of this state of being is a journey of spiritual growth, one can move toward it with the help of certain practices. Personally, I find a particular meditation technique very useful. I call it '*Silent Sitting*'. I close my eyes and let any thoughts, images, or sounds populate my mental canvas.

I do not try to focus or concentrate on anything. I simply let my thought stream flow. Some of the images are disturbing and random. Others are funny. Some are sad. They transition like a slideshow. At some point, the images disappear, and I stare into nothingness.

At this stage, a feeling of unbridled love envelops me. It is a love for all things and for all people. It is a love that celebrates every existence equally. It is a love that is spared from the pain of loss. When I emit this raging love, I am filled with an incredible sensation of happiness that is impossible to describe in words. It is the happiness that flows from attachment with detachment.

Question 13

Is Our Destiny Pre-written?

*H*as our future been written for us, or can we shape it ourselves? Are we bystanders to fate or do we play a crucial role in its working?

We have all asked these questions at some stage because we think that the outcomes of our actions are so uncertain that we need an emotional coping mechanism to handle them. Depending on what we believe, we use this mechanism to protect ourselves from pain or the mere possibility of it.

Destiny is the cycle of reactions and consequences of our actions. When we complete an act, we receive a response from the environment. This reaction is delivered based on our intention. If our intent is authentic and comes from a place of care, empathy or higher purpose, we will receive a positive response, even if things do not turn out as we planned. On the other hand, if our intent is inauthentic and driven by lust, greed, or other negative vibes, we will receive a negative response from our surroundings, even when the result may appear to be favorable. Here are examples of the above scenarios.

A soldier shoots an enemy combatant and kills him. Instead of getting punished and suffering from guilt or depression, he gets a hero's welcome. His community celebrates his actions, and he feels happy within. He suffers no adverse consequences of any sort despite taking a human life because he has diligently followed his personal duty of defending the country. In contrast, a person who kills another and robs him of his wealth is eventually arrested and sentenced to death. Additionally, he experiences abuse at the hands of his prison inmates and the ignominy of being blacklisted by his community.

In these cases, we can see that the response to one's actions is not commensurate with the act itself but with the intent that underpins the act. Therefore, we can conclude that the cycle of action, reaction, and consequences is based on the positivity of one's intention rather than the action itself.

How can we explain the common observation that bad things happen to good people?

Whenever a person is born, their body is formed for the first time. However, the soul is reborn in this new shell. That soul first emerged from its cradle—the origin of the Universe—many lifetimes ago. The soul undergoes numerous births, lives, and deaths before it reunites with The One. At the time of an individual's birth, therefore, their soul has already experienced several lives and must experience the consequences of those actions performed in its previous lives. This is why one person may be born into a wealthy, loving family and live in a peaceful country, while another is born on the street and subsequently abandoned.

The boundary conditions of an individual are, therefore, immutable because they have resulted from the deeds in one's past lives. However, are we destined to repeat those same mistakes in our present lives? Are we mere silent spectators with no mental agency? The answer to both questions is a resounding *no*.

While the actions of our past cannot be reversed, going forward, we have the power to act according to our volition. It is possible to remove those inhibitions that arise as a result of the consequences of our former lives through a process of self-filtration. This involves making sacrifices and surrendering to one's Guru Tatwa. Through this process of filtration, an individual can extricate themselves from the cycle of births and achieve Oneness. Here are two examples of the nature of destiny.

In *Ramayana*, Shri Ram was exiled from his kingdom. This was his destiny—one that he chose. Seen from afar, his fate would seem to be harsh, even hopeless. Yet, while Shri Ram accepted the outcome, he was not prepared to reconcile himself to the misery and emotional breakdown that could have been the norm in his future. He used the period of his exile to filter himself from barriers and develop his inner self. Consequently, he became the revered Lord Ram.

In *Mahabharata*, Arjun—the renowned warrior and third Pandava brother—was exiled from his kingdom with his siblings for 13 years. During this period, he was invited to the palace of Indra, his father. There, he met a celestial nymph called Urvashi. She was impressed by his talents and professed her love for him. However, he rebuffed her advances because she had once been the wife of King Pururavas, his ancestor. Thus, she was like a mother to him. Insulted by the rejection, Urvashi cursed him to live as a eunuch for the rest of his life—a curse that Indra reduced to a year. Stripped of their sexual identity, most people in this situation would have been distraught and devastated. Not Arjun. Remaining emotionally detached from his masculinity, he accepted the curse as an opportunity to evolve. Thus, he welcomed the transformation from a handsome warrior to a eunuch, Brihannala. In his new avatar, he resided at King Virata's Matsya Kingdom, where he taught his daughter, Uttara, music and dance. Far from being dejected and trapped in a shell, Arjun made full use of his time in Matsya and led an enriching life.

Thus, returning to the question, 'Is our fate pre-written?'; the answer is *Yes*. However, we have the inner power to shape it.

Use this force with love and positivity. You will receive Nature's magnanimous embrace.

Question 14

How Can We Preserve the Innocence of Childhood?

Childhood is a time of innocence. It is filled with vivid and indelible memories. Some of these are magical, sparking joy and positivity, lingering in our minds forever. Others are dark and bitter, leaving behind a sour trail of negativity. Notwithstanding their color, childhood experiences always leave a permanent mark on our consciousness. Their aftereffects go a long way in molding our character, personality, and outlook toward life and in setting us on course to being who we are. Here are a few examples of the innocence of childhood.

Nachiketa, the legendary sage, was very innocent as a child. His father, Vajashravasa, had commenced an offering of his possessions to the gods. However, Nachiketa noticed that his father was only donating infirm cows. Wanting the best of offerings to be placed before the gods, Nachiketa asked Vajashravasa if he, himself, could be donated. In a fit of rage, his father said that he would offer his son to Yamaraj, the God of Death. Innocent Nachiketa then traveled to Yamaraj's home in order to offer himself. However, the God of Death was absent. So, Nachiketa waited at his doorstep without food or water. Three days later, when Yamaraj returned and saw the young boy, he apologized profusely for making him wait for so long. He told Nachiketa that there was no need to offer himself. Instead, he engaged with the boy on the question of life after death. Subsequently, Nachiketa returned to his father, significantly evolved.

Maharaja Ranjit Singh was the King of Punjab (now in Pakistan) in the nineteenth century. He was renowned for his benevolence and passion for life. One day, when he was returning home, he was struck on the head by a stone. At that time, a few children had been throwing stones at a mango tree to dislodge its fruits. One of them had accidentally hurled the projectile. Spotting the ruler and his entourage, the kids then beat a hasty retreat. The king sent guards to the nearby village with an order to summon the boys and their parents to court. The affected families were terrified. However, they had no choice but to comply. The next day, the king met the villagers. He not only pardoned the mistake but also offered each of them ₹ 51 along with a platter of sweets. He justified his decision by explaining that trees are hit by stones all the time. Yet, they do not react with anger and hurt the perpetrators. They share their bounty instead. Thus, human beings should aspire to be broad-minded and benevolent like trees. Consequently, he spared innocent children from punishment.

Like us, every creature on the planet—plants, animals, insects—is shaped by its childhood experiences, for good or for bad. Since positive childhood experiences are crucial in the development of Nature's every child, one would think that close attention would be paid to seeding a nurturing environment. Sadly, this is not the case.

Irrespective of the species, most children are presented with an environment that is oppressive, exploitative, and unstimulating. Human kids are thrown into a world rife with division, oppression, and prejudice and are unable to follow their passions, forge meaningful relationships, or develop themselves to their full potential. Millions are forced to toil in factories and sweatshops to make the average adult comfortable.

Plant kids emerge in a world suffocated by greenhouse gases, industrial waste, and deforestation. Very often, they are cruelly plucked from nurseries to make space for concrete jungles of apartment blocks and corporate offices. Animal children come of age in forests and oceans with shrinking habitats, limited food supply, and toxic pollutants. So often, they are turned into food, toys, props, or physical aids for our pleasure and amusement. Notwithstanding their genetic code, the children of Nature are mistreated and ignored around the world, their needs and priorities given short shrift.

Our attitude toward them requires a rapid reset. Unless we do so urgently, the problems confronting us and the planet will become more devastating. Eventually, a time will come when Nature will no longer turn a blind eye to our capriciousness, lust, and intolerance. She will respond to our brutality with commensurate force—spawning hurricanes that will turn our lives upside down, leaving us reeling and panicking.

We can change our attitude toward our children by first recognizing that they are the future. The world belongs to them. They are the ones who will carry our legacy forward. They are the ones who will make a quantum leap in innovation and progress. They own the future. So, it is our responsibility to pave the road for them. If we believe in these precepts, we would take child development very seriously and adopt a holistic approach toward nurturing every child of Nature to its full potential. We would never exploit them. We would never dominate them. We would not throw spanners into their dreams. We would nurture them with seeds of love and fertilizers of knowledge. We would help them evolve their consciousness.

Only then would we shape a Onesome world. A world where all living beings would merge with The One. A world where happiness is a state of mind that is universally attained and perpetually maintained.

Question 15

What Are Dreams?

All of us emerged into the world as conscious beings. At the time of our inception, not only could we decode information that we gathered from our environment through our senses, but we could also feel desire, love, pain, anger, sadness, and so many other emotions. Our innate faculties helped us understand the physical world and stoked our desire to influence it. They also served as media, reminding us of our past life experiences. Visions pertaining to our experiences in the Universe—past and future—are called dreams. We have been experiencing these since infancy.

There are three types of dreams.

- *Type 1 (Past Life)*

These are manifested when we are asleep and are related to our experiences in our previous lives. These memories persist in our consciousness well after our soul has departed one physical vessel to inhabit our current shell. The past life memories often surface in the form of vignettes and elicit an emotional response. These may inspire, torture, or haunt us today, depending on our actions in that life. In some sense, Type 1 dreams represent Nature's response to the intentions that guided our actions in those lives. Therefore, we can justifiably conclude that they represent some portion of our dues from those births.

For instance, Maha Maya, the mother of Buddha, experienced this type of dream when she was pregnant with Gautam. She saw a white elephant with six tusks entering her right side. This was interpreted to mean that she would conceive a child who would become either a world ruler or an enlightened person.

- *Type 2 (Prophetic)*

These dreams pertain to our future. We experience them when we daydream or fantasize about our desires. All of us desire to connect with the One. While we may not be aware of how to achieve a permanent connection, we are all familiar with the feeling of satisfaction that flows through our being upon achieving a short-term one. In our minds, we often equate such a connection with the enjoyment of rewards such as fame, wealth, social status, etc. Thus, we conjure visions that showcase a sunny future, one resplendent with multi-colored jewels and sparkling gemstones. Thereafter, these visions galvanize us to embark on further pursuits.

- *Type 3 (Visionary)*

These dreams are what we experience when we are fully conscious. This is when we visualize a goal without being attached to its outcome. When we enter this state, we feel tremendously self-assured and confident about taking on challenges. We feel serene, empowered, and in control of our destiny.

For instance, Chanakya, the master political strategist in the Mauryan era, harbored a dream of an Undivided India *(Akhand Bharat)*. He visualized this idea into a concrete and implementable master plan. Thereafter, he seeded it in the hearts and minds of Chandragupta Maurya. Consequently, imbued with a sense of purpose, the latter overthrew the powerful Nandi dynasty of Pataliputra and established the Maurya Empire across the nation. Therefore, this type of dream is a template for action that can bring about impactful change.

What is the role of dreams in evolving our consciousness?

Dreams provide us with a guide to filter the barriers, a map to scripting our journey in this life, and a compass to stay on course. Past life dreams give us clues to correct, redress, or improve upon our actions from previous lives; Prophetic dreams imbue us with a sense of resolve to embark on a journey to follow our purpose; and Visionary dreams endow us with the serenity and inner balance to plan and concretize the path that we wish to tread.

Irrespective of the type of dream we experience, we must keep in mind that they exist for one purpose—to evolve our consciousness.

Question 16

Why Must We Create?

For the greater part of our lives, we seem to be overtly focused on consumption. We are often so consumed with meeting our fundamental needs that we perceive the acquisition or possession of things as the ultimate purpose of life. We are so obsessed with comfort and security that we tend to become lazy. We do not give anything back to Nature—the Divine Entity—that nourishes and enriches us. Consequently, we feel disconnected from everything and everyone, even from ourselves.

While there is nothing wrong with consumption per se, it behoves us to note that, through this route, we only absorb energy for our individual gratification. Consumption is just one small aspect of a happy life. For long-term fulfillment, we must deepen our connection with the Universe. To do that, we must harness and transmit positive energy to the environment. We must create.

Creation is the gifting of our positive energy to the Universe. It is the culmination of our efforts to connect with The One. Through the creation process, we come closer to the origin of the Universe, expand our consciousness, and experience deep fulfillment.

How does a creation take shape? How does the process expand our consciousness?

When we think of creation, we instinctively visualize an activity, e.g., painting, writing, dancing, sex, etc. Most of us feel that we must engage in a certain type of activity to create something. We forget that these are all different roads that help us reach the same destination—the origin of the Universe—and that there are infinite number of such paths. Through our preferred method, we can access our deepest thoughts and feelings. This allows us to sync our consciousness with The One, harness positive energy, and shape our creation.

A poet might tap her pain of emotional abandonment to compose a poignant sonnet. A painter may etch an idyllic hamlet that he toured with his family on a childhood vacation. A photographer may recognize her grandmother's face on a mountain lion's and strive to capture it for posterity. A couple may explore the vision of a world they had seen in a dream during a passionate session of lovemaking. A guru may feel the presence of a spirit from the future when imparting wisdom to his disciple. Whichever the mode of expression, what is common to them all is the process of connecting with the Ultimate via one's inner world of thoughts and feelings.

Upon achieving a connection, the creator will then experience the joy of being in the moment. In this state of presence, the individual will feel every spark of energy exchanged between them and Nature. Numerous thoughts, feelings, and questions will well up internally. These will not hit a dead brick wall of judgment, causing frustration or anguish. On the contrary, they will elicit responses from the Universe that will fill them with appreciation, wonderment, and a feeling of progress.

The poet will recall a single, pivotal utterance by her father before he had abandoned her to pursue a life with another family. That remark would open a window in her subconsciousness, allowing her to witness a cathartic downpour of her loneliness.

This passionate yet detached observation of her feelings would lead her toward greater self-realization, empathy, and, possibly, forgiveness for her demon.

The painter will smell the musty odor of the hamlet—a threadbare enclosure where he had enjoyed a game of catch with his two long-lost siblings. That scent would remind him of the joys of friendship, community, and brotherhood— values that had gotten lost over time.

The photographer will remember that time in her teenage years when her grandmother organized her first tour of an animal preserve and explained the nuances of animal life and upkeep—based on four decades of experience as the director of the encampment. The sight would enthuse her with belief in a spirit guide and dispel her faithlessness.

The lovers' hearts will burst with passion and unbridled excitement like those of pioneers' before they charted their journey to virgin lands. Like their predecessors, they would be filled with boundless optimism for a life without limits. These feelings would then translate to a nurturing and liberal style of parenting and a relationship based on the bedrock of trust, care, and openness.

The Guru's heart will be filled with joy upon seeing his disciples learning, growing, and actualizing the qualities that he saw in them. Their love for each other will grow manifold with each experience of filtration and sacrifice.

The most powerful example of creation is the facilitation of one's evolution by another. Here are a few stories that illustrate this awesome transformation.

In *Mahabharata*, Dronacharya and Arjun enjoyed a special relationship as guru and disciple. Dronacharya, the master of the military arts, trained every Pandava and Kaurava in the art of warfare. However, Arjun was his most devoted student. He absorbed Dronacharya's lessons with complete dedication. He conquered every challenge with discipline and mindfulness. Consequently, he became a master warrior with an impressive array of skills and qualities that would lead his family to victory in the epic war of Kurukshetra.

Parashuram, the sixth avatar of Vishnu, was a supreme warrior and the Guru of Bhishma and Dronacharya. He was a devotee of Lord Shiva. It was the latter who schooled him in the art of warfare. On achieving mastery, Parashuram was awarded an axe-like weapon for his achievements. Thereafter, he was unbeatable in battles.

Narendranath Dutta (1863–1902) was the chief disciple of the nineteenth-century Indian mystic, Thakur Ramkrishna. The latter introduced him to the philosophy of *Advaita Vedanta*, a core tenet of Hinduism. Additionally, he shaped Narendranath's personality and inspired him to take up the mission of service for humanity. Thakur Ramkrishna's teachings spurred Narendranath's transformation from a precocious kid to a sage (Swami Vivekananda) and led to the subsequent propagation of a hitherto unknown and ancient philosophy around the world.

These stories show that the power of creation is not limited to the production of goods, services, or other types of assets. It also encompasses the development of a being via the transmission of energy from guru to disciple.

During the process of creation, a plethora of emotions and thoughts are catalyzed in the creator, causing them to enter a state of connectedness and experience deep satisfaction. They will then convey this feeling in the form of a creative expression. This could be an object, an idea, or even a life. The expression may receive a positive or a negative endorsement. Even more so, it may be greeted with indifference. Notwithstanding the outcome, the creator's satisfaction levels will hardly be diluted because they will be inundated with the joy of the moment. They will then radiate their positivity to the Universe, galvanizing others with the power and majesty of their creation.

Question 17

How Can We Reinvent
Ourselves?

Every being in the Universe—living or nonliving—undergoes a process of birth and renewal. At the time of its birth, energy from previous lives intermingles with that of its immediate surroundings—people and Nature— and results in its formation. At that time, the being is endowed with three sets of qualities: *Sattva Guna* (virtue, harmony, construction, etc.), *Rajas Guna* (ego, passion, activity, etc.), and *Tamas Guna* (inertia, imbalance, disorder, vice, etc.)

Each characteristic is like a thread that runs through the being. The ratio of these threads differs for everyone. However, no being is exclusively composed of any one or two of them. During the course of the being's lifespan, these qualities are expressed through various actions and thoughts at different times and situations. The state of mind of the being during the performance of its acts determines its rewards or penalties in the future. These could be earned or levied either in the present life or the ones to follow. Therefore, one's destiny is predetermined to a great extent, but not completely. Even though fate is pre-written, it is possible for a being to shape it by filtering itself. Through this process, the being evolves its consciousness and brings the three aforementioned qualities in balance. This method of inner restitution is known as *Tandava*.

Tandava is a process of self-appraisal whereby a being evaluates itself. It first investigates its energy composition and discovers the proportion of qualities within it. Thereafter, it undertakes a process of filtration whereby it detaches itself from all these characteristics. Subsequently, it is able to alter its energy balance and join the Universe in a renewed state. Here is a story from the *Vishnu Purana* that depicts Tandava.

The objective of the Samudra Manthan (the churning of the Ocean of Milk) was to uncover the nectar of immortality. During the process, several objects were produced. Not all were benign. The deadliest output was a poison that threatened the existence of every creature in the Universe. The emergence of the toxin was a sudden and unexpected phenomenon. It shocked everyone, sending them scrambling for help. The sheer havoc wrought by this hazardous, unanticipated specter plunged the entire operation into uncertainty. There was a strong possibility that the entire process would have to be abandoned, and the Universe, as a result, would be imperiled. However, the participants in the Samudra Manthan stuck to their guns because they were committed to the goal of discovering the elixir—the grand prize. So, they sought help from the wise to get past the poison. After countering this challenge successfully, they learned that such difficulties are part and parcel of any exercise and must be welcomed as opportunities for growth. Stirred by this mindset, they suspended their fears and judgments. They continued to churn the ocean with a renewed attitude and openness, bravely witnessing the emergence of new objects. In the end, a vast array of valuables emerged to the surface, culminating with the most valuable prize—the nectar.

The story flies in the face of the popular understanding of Tandava as an act of destruction. We picture Lord Shiva dancing atop Mount Kailasha, hailing fire and brimstone on Earth, instantly incinerating it. This portrait seems to suggest that Tandava is an inherently violent act. Nothing is further from the truth. In the Samudra Manthan, a series of unpredictable, violent challenges led to the discovery of the nectar. To resolve these problems, the participants had to filter themselves from inhibitions. Thus, an inherently chaotic exercise fostered a breakneck evolution.

Since energy is neither created nor destroyed, the allusion of demolition or death is incorrect. Rather, we should look at the end of a life cycle as its renewal. This is a stage when all qualities are nullified and recycled to shape a new consciousness. The ultimate self-appraisal process.

We all fear the end as the decimation of happiness. It is not. The end is the beginning of a new dawn. A new era. The rebirth of consciousness.

Question 18

Why Do We Harbor
Friendship and Enmity?

Throughout our lives, we interact with many people. These interactions are collaborative exchanges involving various activities, conversations, sharing, etc. Through these dealings, we exchange energy with one another. Durable ties are established only when positivity is regularly expressed and reciprocated. With an increase in the frequency of interactions, trust and intimacy grow stronger, and the relationship evolves into friendship.

Friendship is a positive feeling that we experience toward another being. The feeling compels us to express our hearts and deepen our connection with the Universe. We behave in a loving manner with that entity. This makes them feel intimately connected with us. We would not have felt positively toward them unless we felt the same way about ourselves.

We have a relationship with our inner self—our consciousness—that houses all our memories and emotions. If the relationship with our inner self is positive, we express love to ourselves. This turns us into our very own best friend. Consequently, we share our self-love, making the recipient of our affection happier and cementing our bond.

The ultimate state of friendship is that of deep self-love. In this state, one's self-connection is so strong that they feel integrated with the fabric of the Universe. They feel attached to everything yet detached at the same time. They can absorb both positive and negative energy, but choose to emit only love to their surroundings. In this state of heightened self-awareness, the individual emits love to everyone, undeterred by how the recipient might respond. Thus, friendship can be truly expressed only when one befriends oneself.

However, we often experience instances when we harbor negative feelings toward others, e.g., anger, frustration, sadness, etc. We then vilify a few of these individuals as enemies. Why?

Enmity is the absence of friendship with oneself. The root cause of enmity is the lack of self-awareness, a case in point being the ignorance of one's barriers. Due to this lack of consciousness, one's connection with oneself is weakened. This leads to low self-acceptance and, consequently, negative feelings about oneself. In other words, the relationship of a person with themselves is not friendly but fraught with animosity and ill will. This self-enmity, often stoked by negativity from others, is projected onto the environment in the form of poisonous expressions. Here are examples of how friendship and enmity develop within oneself and are then transmitted externally.

An entrepreneur has suffered a business failure. This setback has fomented negative feelings. He is angry at himself for not rising to his own expectations and is too depressed to undertake a holistic introspection. He then punishes himself by writing himself off. He declares internally that he is not good enough to do business. One day, someone comments that most entrepreneurs fail due to poor planning. This remark hurts the entrepreneur further because it forces him to relive the memory of his self-condemnation. Since he has not acquired self-awareness, the entrepreneur looks at the statement as another stinging rebuke of his talent. Thereafter, he projects his anger onto the critic, painting him as his mortal enemy.

A woman—who has been married for twenty years— finds out that her husband has walked out of the relationship. She is full of grief. To assuage her sorrow, she expresses her emotions through music. After a cathartic spell of creativity, she composes an album with songs that convey her searing pain. Through the process, she realizes that her husband suffers from trauma due to his mother's sudden exit from her marriage. Tormented by emotional abandonment, he had been unconsciously searching for a mother figure to fill his void. His barrier is emotional trauma, the woman learns.

However, she discovers through her music that it is his responsibility to filter himself from it. It is not a role that she is supposed to fill. Enriched with this understanding, she appreciates her qualities, talents, virtues, and ultimately, herself, in a wholesome way. Refusing to be mired in self-blame, she expresses her positivity toward her surroundings by performing in various open-air spaces. One day, the lady meets a close friend of her ex-husband. He is supportive of her ex-husband, who has fed him many disparaging stories about her. Feeling angry, he asks her if she is guilty about driving him away. Flush with love and self-belief, she responds to this acidic question gallantly. "I only want to see him happy. Convey my love to him. I hope he will find what he is looking for," she replies with a smile. Gazing at the woman's radiant expression, the husband's friend realizes that she has undergone a huge change since her breakup. Today, she is in a far, far better place than ever before. Impressed by her transformation and positive mindset, he talks her up in his circle of associates. The resounding endorsement brings her not only busloads of fans but true friends as well.

In *Mahabharata*, Karna came into possession of the deadly *Narayana Astra*—an invincible weapon that could fire hundreds of missiles simultaneously at the enemy. The only way to counter this weapon is through love and submission. Karna wanted to destroy the Pandavas by wielding the Narayana Astra. However, Yogeshwar Krishna taught Arjun that the weapon would be rendered ineffectual if the targets did not harbor enmity in their hearts. Imbibing the lesson, the Pandavas and their men entered a deep meditative state wherein they paid obeisance to the Narayana Astra. In the process, they cleansed their hearts of rage and hate and embraced love, appreciation, and positivity. Consequently, the weapon did not hurt anyone.

Angulimala was a violent brigand who lived in the era of Buddha. He was notorious for killing his victims and advertising his exploits by wearing a garland of fingers. In no uncertain terms, he was an enemy of the people. One day, he happened to encounter Buddha. Angulimala wanted to kill the sage and enjoy his 1000th kill. However, Buddha taught him that his thirst for blood stemmed from a restless, unsatisfied spirit. To attain happiness, Angulimala needed to control his desires. The murderer introspected and acknowledged the truth in Buddha's words. Thereafter, he abandoned the path of violence and enmity and became a devout disciple.

These examples demonstrate how the presence or absence of friendship with oneself can lead to the externalization of these sentiments. Thus, it is important to be self-aware by being fully present in the moment. This self-consciousness will keep us in good stead every time we find ourselves in a social situation. We will draw from our awareness, not get adversely affected by how others behave, and not react negatively. On the contrary, we will behave with them as we would behave with ourselves—with respect, empathy, kindness, and a million other emotions fired from the canon of positivity—a bosom friend of the Universe.

Question 19

Is Rebellion the Right Way to Bring About Change?

There were times when we felt angry at people for treating us unfairly or inhumanely. During these moments, we were so upset that we labeled the whole world unjust. Our minds buzzed with thoughts on how to change the imperfections in the environment and in the hearts of people. Some of these thoughts were violent—even hell-bent on wreaking havoc and waging battles. Deep inside, we felt ashamed for harboring such ill will. However, our rage provided us with the justification to cling to our beliefs. We started believing, even adoring, our self-image of the rebel—a person committed to changing society by punishing the villains. A warrior with the single-minded mission to enforce rectitude.

Rebellion is the forceful path of bringing change to one's environment. It involves imposing one's values or rule book on the system with the aid of one's followers. This initiative is galvanized by the rebel's lust to achieve a specific outcome—power.

Rebellion is like a one-way address delivered by the change agent to the public. A lecture without a Q&A session. A forum lacking opportunities for discussion, debate, and dissent. Bereft of the subtleties of dialog, the rebel camp employs authoritarian methods to stamp their principles and erase all vestiges of opposing ideas. This is why rebellion polarizes society into groups of believers and nonbelievers. Moreover, it is an autocratic way of bringing about change. Hence, in the long run, it is unsustainable.

Notwithstanding the demerits of rebellion, it often appears to be the only viable way of changing the system. This is because authorities and gatekeepers of the system are generally concerned with preserving the status quo to secure their benefits. As a result, they often resist change. Regardless of their comfort factor, it is always important for a system of governance to upgrade and modernize.

Given that the path of rebellion is so divisive, how does one bring about transformation in an inclusive manner?

Path-making is the transformation of a system via constructive means. It requires one to jettison force. On the contrary, its primary forces for leading change are openness, creativity, and collaboration. While rebellion is driven by the change agent's lust for certain personal gains, path-making is spurred by their need to merge with The One.

Path-making is like a brainstorming session conducted by the change agent to generate ideas for betterment. Since most successful engagements of this sort invite contributions from a diverse pool of participants, the change agent must proactively rope in contributors of all stripes, even those who are change-averse and labeled as the 'enemy'. Thus, in the world of path-making, there are no opponents. Only contributors and implementors. This is why path-making is a more inclusive, constructive way of bringing about change than rebellion and it is more likely to lead to more sustainable outcomes.

Examples of rebellion and path-making can be found in the novel *Goliath of Shenzhen* by Aritra Sarkar. In this book,

Di, the protagonist, leads his rural community in an uprising against the Chinese government for evicting them from the village that has been their home for generations. They mount a revolt by building and commanding a battle robot. Their intention is to incinerate the Chinese army before setting the whole of China ablaze. However, the revolt is ultimately squashed by deceit, intimidation, and politics. Subsequently, a vanquished Di introspects on his failure and realizes that the betterment of his people could be brought about by rural development, not war. He realizes that his true calling lies in building technology to help villages progress. Thereafter, he partners with the Chinese government to build a range of industrial robots that transform the agri-economy. In the process, he turns into an industrial maven who leaves a lasting positive impact on society.

The Hippie Movement, which began in the US in the 1960s as a protest against organized religion and the political system, is an example of rebellion against widely-practiced social mores. It flourished for two decades, giving birth to the legendary mantra 'Make love, not war'. However, members took this statement literally and prioritized the satisfaction of their physical and material needs over the growth of their consciousness. As the culture of material excess and hedonism began to spread in the hippie communes like wildfire, the souls of members began to get disconnected from the origin of the Universe. Thereafter, ego started to rule their decisions, violating the original spirit and intentions of the movement. Unsurprisingly, the hippie culture ebbed away and never became the positive, world-changing force that it was expected to be.

On the other hand, here are a few examples of path-making that resulted in positive outcomes.

Raja Ram Mohan Roy (1772–1833) was a social reformer from Bengal who founded the organization *Brahmo Samaj*. This institution championed women's rights in India during the late eighteenth century by crusading against entrenched social customs such as the *Sati Pratha* (immolation of widows), polygamy, and child marriage.

The Chipko Andolan was a forest conservation movement that began in Mizoram in 1873. Initiated as a nonviolent protest, this movement went on to inspire many environmental protests around the world. It was the first environmental movement in India to stir civil society by using the original slogan, 'Ecology is the Permanent Economy'. Through protests that employed Satyagraha methods, the Chipko Andolan drew attention to the issues of the destruction of livelihoods and deforestation in the country. Even today, it remains the benchmark for nonviolent environmental movements in the world.

Judging from these stories, it can be easily concluded that path-making is the right way of bringing about change because it is inclusive and based on empathy, innovation, and tolerance.

So, if you ever feel compelled to be a change agent, embrace these positive values. You will see your vision sparkle to life.

Question 20

When Do We Need to Break the Rules?

Since birth, we have seen the world operate on a system of rules. For instance, let us take the physical world. It is governed by the principles of physics, mathematics, biology, etc. Other spheres of the world are no different. Civil society is administered through constitutional rules and various social norms. Interpersonal relationships function on assumptions and behaviors that underpin religion and ethics. Nothing in the world,—no sphere of life, no being—seems to be exempt from the rule book. Because we inherit these rules from our environment without a viable choice of determination, these guidelines are called *external rules*. For the entirety of our lives, we have to follow them.

How are our lives impacted by the worship of the external rule book?

By adhering to social norms and constitutional laws, we can gain the respect of people and credibility with authorities. By sticking to the rules of the physical world, we can be healthier and less injury prone. By following the practices of our religion, we can feel a sense of inner harmony. This helps us maintain amicable relations. However, while the strict pursuit of the rule book may lead to stable outcomes in one's life, these are by no means a *given*. Very often, people experience undesirable and unintended consequences of puritanical worship.

The rigid regard for social norms, traditions, laws, and customs may invite social stigma should the rules change, and the earlier ones are deemed regressive. The strict abidance to Nature's empirical rules may help one remain safe in the short term. However, the body and mind would be starved of challenges for growth and filtration. As a result, we would be unprepared to deal with black swan events, setbacks, or other unforeseen obstacles. Our obsessive immersion in a value system may lead to moral inflexibility and ego and prevent us from taking hard decisions. Thus, while the absorption of external rules has indeed positive effects on one's consciousness and life satisfaction, equally powerful negatives may arise. Based on this argument, we can conclude that merely following the external rule book is not enough to achieve conscious growth.

The rule book that has been described earlier refers to a set of external rules, both decreed and normative. As stated, these are acquired from our social environment upon birth. Usually, to feel accepted in society, we are compelled to internalize and follow them. Most of us do. Few even go on to become highly conscious, awakened beings. However, the slavish practice of rigidly following external rules will not result in conscious growth beyond self-awareness. To attain supreme consciousness, they must be complemented by personal rules. Here is an example of one's personal code complementing the conventional rule book.

In *Mahabharata*, the Pandavas struggled to find a way to defeat the legendary master of arms, Guru Dronacharya. No carefully calibrated weapon or skilled warrior could penetrate his defenses. Additionally, the code of honesty laid down by their leader, Yudhisthira, appeared to hinder them from mounting an effective response to the Kauravas' deceitful tactics. As the Pandavas scratched their heads helplessly, Yogeshwar Krishna offered an ingenious solution that would help them achieve their combat goals without violating Yudhishthira's rule book. He suggested that the best way to defeat Dronacharya would be to disarm him then kill him. He would lay down his weapons only if he were grief-stricken. The death of his son, Ashwatthama, would be a cause for the same.

Then, Yogeshwar Krishna instructed Bheem to kill an elephant named Ashwatthama and to circulate the rumor that he had killed Dronacharya's son. Onboard the strategy, Bheem killed an elephant by the name of Ashwatthama and then announced to the world that Dronacharya's son had died. A horrified Dronacharya verified the news with the paragon of righteousness and truth, Yudhishthira. The latter replied, "Ashwatthama is dead. But he is an elephant, not your son." Knowing Yudhishthira's penchant for honesty, Yogeshwar Krishna compelled a band of soldiers to blow on conches. The sound drowned out the last sentence, limiting Dronacharya to the words, "Ashwatthama is dead." Finally believing the news, a shattered Dronacharya laid down his weapons and entered a meditative state to discover his son's spirit. At that point, Draupadi's brother, Dhrishtadyumna, killed him.

Like the case above, we often face instances when we feel hamstrung by external rules. It seems that our objectives can be met only if we violate them. However, the example shows that one's personal rules can align with the external rulebook and help us achieve our goals. Thus, everyone should strive to derive their own relevant set of guidelines and principles. The content of the individual rule book is based on one's unique life circumstances. It is composed with the intention of facilitating personal evolution. It is neither driven by the need to revolt against the external rule book nor to support it fervently. Everyone should practice the tenets of their rule book religiously, without deviation, knowing full well that every rule applies equally to oneself as to others. Should the practitioner do so with dedication and diligence, they would assimilate the qualities of inner discipline and devotedness on their own terms. Thereafter, they could leverage these traits and achieve a state of deep connectedness with The One and a state that is beyond the three-dimensional world of needs, relationships, and achievements. To achieve this level of consciousness, therefore, it is essential for the individual rule book to deviate from the external one. Here is an example of the same deviation.

Chandragupta Maurya (321–297 BC), founder of the Mauryan Empire in India, was embroiled in a costly, two-year war with the Greek emperor, Seleucus. Instead of extending the battle, Chandragupta decided to end it by marrying Seleucus' daughter, thereby entering into an alliance with the Greeks. This was a highly unusual practice at that time, even more so among nobles, who were always expected to wed within strict ethnocultural lines. Notwithstanding the social rules of marriage, Chandragupta realized that the greater good would be accomplished if they were to set them aside.

This example shows that an individual's internal rule book may compel them to make some decisions that are socially unacceptable, even illegal. It may coerce a person to forsake their relationships or even flirt with death. While such actions may seem extreme or misguided, these are necessary processes for one's inner filtration to achieve Oneness. Here, it must be emphasized that such initiatives are not necessary for one to become conscious or awakened. The diligent pursuit of external rules is sufficient for this purpose. However, to go beyond awareness and achieve Oneness, it is important to follow a personal rule book.

To sum up, we need rules for direction and discipline. To attain consciousness, it is sufficient to follow the rule book that has been handed down to us. However, to attain Oneness, we must create and follow our personal rule book. Do not look at rules as chains. Consider them as tools for self-improvement.

Question 21

Is Gender Purely about Biology?

Since time immemorial, gender roles have been etched on stone tablets. Women are supposed to stay at home and take care of the kids. Men are supposed to earn bread and butter. Marriage and the nurturing of children traditionally fall within the domain of male-female relationships. We have all learned these stereotypes.

Although they have proved to be highly durable, they are negative for growth. The participation of women in the workplace, especially in the upper echelons of organizations, continues to trail men. Men are discouraged by society and their detractors, including family members, the media, and their peers, from splitting household responsibilities with women. Individuals with unconventional gender identities—who are neither obviously masculine nor feminine, i.e., transgender or nonbinary—are still not accepted by society. In fact, an individual's gender identity is viewed in such a monochromatic light that it feels like an external barrier to the evolution of consciousness.

Gender is the signature of our qualities and Nature in our consciousness. To elucidate this point, I would like to cite an analogy from human anatomy. Blood and water. These substances are vital for the normal functioning of the body. Similarly, masculinity and femininity flow within our consciousness like sentient rivers of sedimentary qualities. The sediments borne by these rivers include nurturing, compassion, resilience, strength, and aggression. These traits can be segregated into two distinct streams—the rivulets of masculinity and femininity. The waters of these brooks flow both separately and concurrently throughout our existence. The continuous divergence and merger of these tributaries reflect the fluidity of our gender identity. This example suggests that masculinity and femininity are qualities that exist within every being.

How do gender identity and sexual preference evolve?

One's anatomical gender has no relation to one's gender identity. It is possible for a person to have an abundance of masculine qualities and to thus hanker for feminine traits. This person may or may not be a biological male. However, they would view themselves as male. They would desire a partner with feminine traits to complete those aspects of themselves that are missing. Thus, sexual preference is directly linked to one's gender identity, not anatomy. Homosexuality and transgenderism can now be understood through this prism.

The sexual preference for one's biological gender stems from the desire to achieve a union of souls. This is the amalgamation of masculine and feminine qualities that is needed to achieve a spiritual fusion. For example, consider two biological women. One has a surfeit of masculine qualities. She is actually a 'he' in spirit. She is searching for a partner with abundant feminine traits so as to spiritually unite. That person may be of any anatomical dispensation.

Now, let us take the example of a transgender individual. He or she is biologically intersex, i.e., having both male and female sex organs. Moreover, his or her composition of masculine-feminine traits is evenly balanced. This means that gender identity is not constant, and consequently, sexual preference is fluid. In this scenario, the transgender person may be equally disposed sexually toward individuals who identify themselves as male, female, both, or neither. A common thread that ties these examples together is the purpose of sex. It is not a mere act of procreation. It is a spiritual union. Even if the physical act of sex does not yield a child, the generation of energy is tantamount to an act of creation that is equivalent to reproduction. Here are a few examples that elucidate the true meaning of gender as a stream of qualities, not biology.

Laxmibai, the Queen of Jhansi (1828–1858), was raised like every other woman of her time. She was groomed in the arts and graces of royalty and to be a silent consort of the future king. She was educated at home, taught to read, and write. Notwithstanding her traditional feminine upbringing, she chose to forge her own path which was not the norm. From an early age, she showed interest in conventional masculine activities like horseback riding, fencing, and shooting. After the Sepoy Rebellion broke out, the Rani of Jhansi joined the resistance against the British in 1858. She led her troops against the imperialist forces, commandeered by Sir Hugh Rose. She even fought against the British soldiers while riding horseback with her child, Damodar Rao, tied to her back. Despite her valiant resistance, she was killed in battle. Her story, however, inspired future revolutionaries to take on the might of the British Empire. Even to this day, her tale inspires women to break free from the stereotypical roles that have been assigned to them in society.

In *Mahabharata*, Shikhandi, the reincarnation of Amba, was a transgender warrior. He was born Shikhandini, a woman.

However, as a child, she switched genders and became a man. Famed for his prowess in the art of military combat, Shikhandi joined the Pandavas in their quest to restore justice to Hastinapur. In the Kurukshetra War, he fought alongside them and was instrumental in causing the death of Bhishma.

The nineteenth century saint, Thakur Ramkrishna, had always been in touch with his feminine side. He often spent time with women in close, platonic situations—an aberration in those days—because he made them feel comfortable, safe, and seen. When he assumed the *Madhura Bhav*—the position of the lover as she approaches God—he dressed in feminine clothing and imitated feminine behavior. For a few days in his life, Thakur Ramkrishna even followed the rules of Yogeshwar Krishna's *Sakhi Sampraday* (community of friends). During that time, he acquired feminine qualities and even experienced the menstrual cycle.

On the basis of the above arguments. We can safely conclude that while biology is fixed and one-dimensional, gender identity is fluid and complex. This aspect must be appreciated when we think about gender roles in society. Instead of blindly reflecting our biases that are rooted in physical appearance, we should choose gender roles that embody our inner selves. So, if you feel pigeonholed on account of your gender, just remember one thing—how you see yourself is far more important than how others see you.

Gender is a state of mind, not a biological reality.

Question 22

What Does It Mean to Be a Parent?

We all have strong feelings about our parents. These emotions have accumulated within us over the course of many years and through a multitude of experiences. Experiences when we would exchange energy via words and deeds. This energy has made us who we are today. Once we came of age, we, too, wanted to be parents. We wanted to step into the shoes of our predecessors. However, are we aware of what it means to be a parent?

Parenthood is the nurturing and germination of one's progeny. The birth of an offspring is the culmination of the expression of love by two partners. The partners may be humans, other living beings, nonliving beings, or The One. Love may be expressed physically or spiritually. Notwithstanding the identity of the partners or the mode of expression of love, the consequent expression leads to the commingling of certain qualities—masculinity, femininity, etc. This causes energy to be exchanged between the entities. The result is an output—a creation. A creation can manifest itself in different forms.

Creation can be tangible. Tangible forms may be living creatures or nonliving beings. A classic example of a living creation is a child. Born from an act of procreation between two living beings, a living child is the resultant of energy exchange due to hormonal secretions. On the other hand, an example of a nonliving child is a painting. Although it appears to be devoid of the liveliness of a living child, it is the product of spiritual 'mating' between a creator and The One. Therefore, it carries the same emotional attachment to the creator and The One as a human child does to its parents.

How does the transfer of energy happen during the expression of love between parents?

When we express our love to someone, we desire to unify with that entity. We sense certain qualities in the being that are missing within us. Through the expression of love, we tap these qualities by exchanging our energies. As a result, we co-create something. This may or may not be a child.

Let us take the example of an act of love that does not produce an actual child. In this case, the act would still produce cells composed of the hormonal secretions of the partners. Notwithstanding their composition, visibility, and living status, these fused cells would still trigger a powerful feeling of attachment in the parties. Another example of an act of love that does not lead to biological reproduction is the cultivation of a disciple by a Guru. Here, the Guru expresses their love to The One by guiding and nurturing the apostle's soul. The expression of love leads to the second birth of the individual, which is rendered in the physical form of the disciple.

The expression of parenthood does not depend on the form of the child. Every child requires tending and leadership to develop fully. These two qualities are spoken of as masculine (fatherhood) and feminine (motherhood), respectively. It is known that every child seeks these qualities from their parents.

However, it is not a given that the father would provide mentoring and the mother nurturing. Very often, we see the male figure naturally endowed with feminine qualities. At the same time, the female has a surfeit of masculine traits. In this situation, the woman offers the child the qualities of fatherhood, while the man provides those of motherhood. A nonliving child is no different. It, too, seeks parenthood through the absorption of masculine and feminine energies.

Let us take the example of a laptop, a nonliving being. Once you would have dreamed of owning this object. You wished that someday you would possess one. You expressed your desire unconsciously to The One. This led to a lively dialog of ideas and eventually an expression of your passion. At that point, The One became your lover. You then exchanged your energy by connecting with The One through your passion. Thus, your child—the laptop—was born in your mind. The One then infused your idea into the shell of a nonliving being. Thereafter, you went to a store and gravitated toward a laptop that closely embodied the idea you had spawned in your consciousness. Subsequently, you bought the object. It then became your child.

Now, you have to look after it and direct it in the same way in which you would take care of a human child. To express fatherhood qualities, you must install adequate memory, storage space, and firewalls. To express motherhood, you must handle it gently, not press its keys too hard, make sure that the cache is cleared regularly, update the antivirus software frequently, and clean the screen often to ensure that your child leads a hygienic life. Should you express your love through the multifaceted qualities of parenthood, the laptop would evolve and be happy. Consequently, it would perform well and lead a long, fulfilling life. Here are a few more examples of the diverse qualities of parenthood.

John Wright, a New Zealand national cricketer in the 1980s, was inducted as the coach of the Indian cricket team in 2000. Prior to his appointment, Indian players were infamous for their sub-par fitness levels and indiscipline as compared to the members of leading international teams. This was the main reason for Team India's underperformance in foreign conditions. Wright formed a close partnership with India's captain, Sourav Ganguly. They instituted programs in physical fitness, agility, and placed great emphasis on individual discipline in the form of regular net practice, punctuality, and attendance. This much-welcomed dose of fatherhood in the coaching style brought about a transformation in the team's fortunes. In 2001, India scripted a remarkable comeback against the top-ranked Australian team and went on to win the series. In 2003, they drew against Australia in their own backyard. In the same year, India memorably defeated Team Pakistan in Pakistan. John Wright's approach to coaching is a wonderful case study of the expression of fatherhood.

Dr Abdul Kalam, the 11th President of India, is regarded as the mother of India's satellite and missile program. He birthed India's first indigenous satellite program in the 1980s. This initiative was the precursor to the nation's ballistic missile program that yielded the missiles—Agni and Prithvi. In 1998, he nurtured the country's nuclear program and its top scientific talent. His leadership was responsible for the successful Pokhran 2 tests in 1998, establishing India as a leading nuclear power. He is an exemplar of motherhood in the field of scientific administration.

To conclude, parenthood is not an action to be performed but rather a state of mind to be attained that is conducive for inculcating a range of qualities required for fostering others. These younglings may take different forms—human, nonhuman, or something intangible. They may be biological or spiritual. However, there is a need that binds them all—the need to be loved, treasured, and nurtured. The golden thread of parenthood.

Question 23

Should We Be Afraid of the Future?

Have you ever wanted to know what the future holds for you? Perhaps you are about to sit for a test and desire to know your professional future, i.e., the career you will pursue and the company you will join. Perhaps you are single and want to find out your marital status in ten years. Perhaps your parents are ill, and you want to inquire about the state of their health five years from now. These are the most pressing questions about the future in people's minds. A market has always existed to supply the answers. A thriving, buoyant industry that provides predictions and forecasts on an array of subjects ranging from life-related questions to horse racing. The most popular field that is centered on prediction is astrology.

Astrology is the science of predicting the future of one's life. Its basis is a numerological system that feeds off the movements of celestial bodies such as stars and planets. Several astrological pedagogies are prevalent worldwide. In the typical astrological genre, a prediction is derived using personal inputs such as time and place of birth. Thereafter, life outcomes are generated from recorded data on the motion of stars and planets. There are many people who live in fear and trepidation due to these prophecies. They are afraid that someday they will be robbed of life, limb, or liberty. These individuals become so terrified of the future that they shroud their existence in a constant cloak of fear and anxiety. Naturally, misery follows them everywhere. Notwithstanding your belief in astrological predictions, there is no reason to fear them.

Astrology is concerned with delivering outcomes, not emotions. In other words, a typical forecast will say that you will attain a pot of wealth in five years. However, it will not tell you if you will be happy or unhappy. This is because the outcome is not a choice, but happiness is. This is a huge and significant point!

While our destiny is pre-determined, our state of being, internal mindset, and intentions are our own volition. We have no control over the acquisition or loss of wealth. However, we can choose how to perceive any situation and react to it. Here is an example of the state of being of two people—A and B—after they became unexpectedly wealthy.

A looks at his newly-minted wealth with lust and wants to hoard even more for his personal consumption. He can afford a penthouse apartment in a prime residential neighborhood. Yet, he would like to upgrade to a bungalow so that he can flaunt his achievements.

In contrast, B views her fortune as a golden opportunity to house the downtrodden in her city. She experiences happiness by sharing her wealth with others.

The mindset of the first individual is selfish. The mindset of the second . . . selfless.

A's mindset would eventually repel people with positive intentions but attract the opportunistic and the cunning. Sensing their greed, A would try to protect himself with various security mechanisms. Even though he may safeguard, perhaps even grow his wealth, the mental pressure of constantly watching over his shoulder would turn him fearful and anxious. Subsequently, his satisfaction levels would deplete.

B, on the other hand, would spread love through her actions. Her deeds would be spoken of far and wide. She would unite people in a positive energy chain and benefit continually from it.

In the above example, the life satisfaction levels of the two individuals differ markedly, despite their identical status of wealth. What if the opposite had occurred: A and B experiencing grave misfortune and losing their wealth? Here too, their mindset, not the outcome, would determine their state of happiness.

Because destiny is pre-written, certain outcomes of life, such as nationality, family, race, and health, are determined before birth. We acquired these boundary conditions of life in our previous birth in order to remove barriers and accelerate the growth of consciousness. The role of astrology is to report these occurrences like an information feed. Then, it is up to us to use the events as a springboard to evolution or as a slippery slope to degeneration. Astrology may provide data about our future, but it would not shed light on how we will feel and, subsequently, react. It cannot alter the most durable and unchanging fact about the Universe. Suffering affects the body, not us. Here is an example to demonstrate that astrological predictions are not to be feared, even if the forecast is true.

Gautama Buddha was born in Lumbini, modern Nepal, between the 4th–5th centuries BCE. After his birth, a hermit seer named Asita prophesied that he would either be a saint or a great king. Gautama's father, Suddhodana, wanted him to follow in his footsteps and become a great ruler.

Fearful of the prophecy of sainthood, he went to extreme lengths to shelter the boy from the harsh realities of the world. Gautama grew up in a gilded palace with access to every conceivable material luxury and comfort. The king intended to seclude the prince in the citadel so that he would never be exposed to poverty, disease, and other forms of blight. He could then concentrate on the royal arts without distractions. Fate, however, had different plans for Gautama. One day, he ventured outside the palace in his chariot. There, he spotted an old, sick man lying on the road. That was the first time he had witnessed poverty. Explaining the concept of sickness, his charioteer informed him that there were many ailing individuals in the world. Chastened by this discovery, Gautama embarked on further missions and encountered many more suffering souls. Thereafter, he realized that he had been presented with a sanitized view of the world. Eager to experience reality, he departed from his cosmetic kingdom and started his spiritual journey.

According to this story, the key driver for Gautama's renunciation of the kingdom was his engineered isolation from suffering. Had he been exposed to this reality from an early age, he may have normalized it and grown apathetic to it. In this scenario, he may have chosen the life of a king. However, the actual path he followed, that of spirituality, led him to experience enlightenment, the deepest happiness possible. Hence, his father's fear of the future was unfounded because it did not stop Gautama from developing his consciousness and finding happiness.

To sum up, there is no reason to fear a negative astrological prediction, even if it were to come to pass, or even if we were to find ourselves in a sticky scenario, suffering tremendous pain. Even in such a horrendous, calamitous situation, we can maintain a positive outlook and transcend our suffering. We can overcome our fear of pain.

Pain is necessary for self-improvement. It is an opportunity to grow our consciousness to higher levels. The greater the pain, the greater the opportunity. Do not shy away from it. Embrace it courageously and passionately.

Question 24

Why Is Pain Necessary?

All of us have endured pain. We may have experienced it momentarily or for a long period of time. We may have felt it as a spasm, an ache, or as a deep convulsion. We may have perceived it in the body, the mind, the heart, or throughout our being. Notwithstanding its level, type, or frequency, we would have begged, prayed, and even pleaded to the Universe to stop the torture. Despairingly, we would have asked why it was needed. Of course, after the tortuous spell had run its course, we would have regained our composure and *joie de vivre*. At that time, we would have realized that the pain had ultimately benefited us. However, we never managed to resolve that most fundamental of existential questions—*why is pain necessary?*

Pain is the unpleasant sensation of resistance caused by Nature. It is Her test to help us deepen our consciousness. It is akin to road friction—that vexing discord between a car and the concrete that enhances its strength, flexibility, and agility. Taking another analogy, education, pain is an examination that we must pass to graduate. It is our homework on the subject of conscious development. Given a choice, most people would avoid pain, just as they would forgo exams, even if it meant losing out on great benefits. Nonetheless, all beings have experienced it.

Are we destined to face pain? Do we have to accept it?

Pain is both destined and selected. Every soul undertakes a journey from imbalance to Oneness. On this journey, the soul must travel from its displaced location in the Universe to its origin. The journey takes place over the course of the soul's life, but it may encompass multiple births. In each birth, the soul occupies a physical vessel or body. Between births, the soul undergoes numerous filtrations/examinations to achieve a higher level of consciousness. Upon the death of the vessel, the soul appraises its state of being. It then selects the next set of challenges to reach the higher evolutionary ground. The reborn soul inherits these boundary conditions of life as well as a fresh vessel to inhabit. Thereafter, it continues this spiritual journey of birth and renewal, until eventually, it unites with The One. In the state of Oneness, there is no need for a body. The soul can finally roam freely in its elemental essence. Every soul feels compelled to embark on the journey to Oneness, because it is restless and lost in its present avatar. Hence, the spirit of seeking is engrained in its nature.

This is why every soul voluntarily chooses a set of challenges to advance in conscious development. Like a student who accepts boredom, stress, and anxiety as necessary personal costs to graduate from a course, we too accept pain as our coursework in evolution. Despite the benefits of accepting pain, most of us strive to evade it.

Since pain is destined, any attempt to evade it will fail. However, we have free will to choose whether to accept it or reject it. Should we decide to reject it—as is the wont of so many—we would end up cultivating a mindset that constantly tries to resist pain. A mindset that's in opposition to Nature's grain. By justifying to ourselves that pain is harmful to our well-being, we try to avoid it or blunt its hurtful effects. In those moments, we convince ourselves that our satisfaction level would increase considerably by avoiding pain. Nothing is further from the truth. By avoiding pain, we not only postpone its ultimate onset but also delay our spiritual evolution.

Avoidance is the trap door to the pit of stagnation—an unseen swamp overrun with numerous (and deadlier) monsters of pain. Losing opportunities for filtration and self-improvement, we entrap ourselves in the cycle of karma—birth, action, and consequences. Consequently, we are unable to achieve our evolutionary potential and taste the fruit of spiritual unity. Here are examples that highlight the role of pain as a propeller in our lives.

Ramayana depicts the story of Ahalya, the wife of Gautama Maharishi, widely regarded as the most beautiful woman of her time. Enamored by her beauty, Indra, the King of the Devas, tried to seduce her by assuming the physical form of her husband. Ahalya recognized Indra's subterfuge. Yet, she went along with the ruse because she was attracted to him. Later on, her husband discovered this and cursed her to become a stone sculpture for all eternity, where she suffered in silence and isolation for a long time. She regained her human form only after Shri Ram purified her by touching her feet.

This story is significant not because it is a chronicle of fantastic events. It is noteworthy as an allegory of the experience of pain. Here, Ahalya succumbed to lust through her senses (*Indriya*). The lust could have been directed at a living being (e.g., a man) or a nonliving one (e.g., a flower).

This seduction is represented by the glorious god, Indra. Consequently, she lost her affection for her husband, Gautama Maharishi. Feeling emotionally neglected, he berated her as a coldhearted woman. As a result, she became a wounded soul and suffered from guilt. She emotionally walled herself off from society. The community ostracized her, forcing her to silently endure the pain of isolation for many years. Eventually, she found solace with Shri Ram. Soothed by his motivational words, she surrendered to him by baring her soul. He encouraged her to express her bottled emotions. Thereafter, she gave herself fully to him and transformed into one of his most ardent devotees. In her new avatar, she experienced joy and connectedness like never before.

Maharana Pratap Singh (1540–1597), the King of Mewar, ceded the capital city of Chittorgarh to Akbar's Mughal forces in 1576. Wounded and humiliated, he sought refuge in the nearby Aravalli hills. In the deep wilderness of the mountains, he nursed his physical and emotional wounds and plotted a rousing comeback. In 1582, his plan came to fruition after he attacked and occupied a key Mughal stronghold, Dewar. After that successful incursion, he engineered several conquests of important Mughal citadels. By 1585, he had recovered a large part of Mewar. Moreover, his revolutionary efforts ensured that the regional economy had recovered considerably from the Mughal-induced depression.

The *Vishnu Purana* tells the story of a Vishnu devotee named Dhruva. When he was five, he tried to sit on his father's lap. However, his jealous stepmother prised him away, saying that he was unworthy and that only God could give him that privilege. He should go and ask him for permission, she remarked cruelly. Deprived of his father's love, Dhruva was disheartened. However, he was hell-bent on gaining his affection. So, he went into the forest to search for God. During the course of his journey, he underwent months of hardship. He had to survive for long periods without food and water. He had to learn the art of meditation and penance. After six months of intense pain, Vishnu finally appeared before him. A delighted Dhruva requested that he be granted a chance to devote his life to the worship of Lord Vishnu. Impressed by his devotion, Vishnu blessed him and granted Dhruva a place in the firmament as the pole star after his death. Thankful and overjoyed, Dhruva returned to his kingdom and was received with great affection by his father.

These examples underscore the fact that pain always surfaces in our lives for a reason. So, when you experience it, tell yourself that it is you who selected it as a growth challenge in the first place. If the pain is tantamount to suffering—excruciating and prolonged—it is because you wanted to deepen your conscious development. The deeper the experience, the greater the benefit. This is why we must embrace pain with open arms.

Question 25

Must We Be Tolerant?

We live in a world where it is difficult to be heard. Wherever we go, we see people arguing with each other in a rude and combative way, refusing to listen to or acknowledge others' views. Their opinions seem to be hardcoded in their minds. Nothing, neither facts nor contrary evidence, can relax their ego. Quite often, we see the disagreements degenerating into verbal brawls, shouting matches, and slang fests, vitiating the atmosphere and polluting it with disrespect. Not for nothing that scholars refer to our times as the Age of Intolerance.

Tolerance is the respect of the views and values of others. It is a quality that enables us to listen to others without judgments and give their views due regard. It is an important trait to inculcate in our journey to Oneness.

By cultivating this quality, we can engage with each other mindfully and in a peaceful manner. Gone will be the days, filled with anger, stress, and anxiety from the pressure of defending our values. Tolerance would be a handy tool to manage conflict and foster cooperation. While the benefits of tolerance at an individual level are like gold beads, at a societal level, they are platinum mines. Here are examples that highlight the value of this quality at both social and personal levels.

Prithviraj Chauhan (1166–1192) was the ruler of the Chahamana dynasty in northwestern India.

He was legendary for his acceptance of other people, value systems, and ways of living. This tolerance was exemplified by his acceptance of the Sufi preacher, Khwaja Moinuddin Chishti. In 1190, the fakir responded to the Prophet's call and traveled to Ajmer, the capital of Prithviraj Chauhan's kingdom. There, he attracted a huge following across social strata— wealthy and peasant, young and old—through his lessons on nonviolence, love, and the pursuit of happiness.

Initially, Prithviraj's close associates were suspicious of the philosopher and wanted the king to banish him. However, Prithviraj wanted to understand why the fakir's teachings appealed to the masses. So, he decided to give Chisti an open, non-judgmental hearing. After the meeting, he was satisfied that Chisti's teachings were neither subversive nor dangerous, but peaceful and inclusive. Subsequently, he allowed the fakir to live and practice freely in his land. After Chisti's death in 1236, a shrine was built in Ajmer and dedicated to him. The dargah was even protected by Prithviraj Chauhan's sons. A beacon of religious tolerance, this shrine is visited by the faithful—Hindus and Muslims—to this day.

Abdul Rahim (1556–1627) was a poet who lived in India during the reign of the Mughal emperor, Akbar. He was famous for his Hindi couplets, known as *dohas*. Although he was Muslim, Rahim accepted and imbibed the values, icons, and tenets of Hindu culture. The assimilation of Hinduism into his consciousness is evident in the following lines from his doha, '*Chitrakoot mein rami rahe*':

> *Chitrakoot me rami rahe rahiman avadhnaresh*
> *japer bipada parat hai voh avat es des*

(The suffering must visit Chitrakoot
This is where Ram, King of Ayodhya, lives.
He will remove everyone's pain and restore the zest
for life.)

This couplet is highly significant in its representation of inter-faith tolerance. Rahim used to pray on the banks of Chitrakoot—a pilgrimage spot in Madhya Pradesh that Shri Ram had visited during his exile. He was so spiritually enmeshed with the teachings of Shri Ram that during meditation he could feel Shri Ram inhabiting his consciousness.

The stories clearly underscore the importance of tolerance in shaping a better world. Tolerance is the prerequisite for a happy world because it is the glue that binds the positive traits of camaraderie and trust into a deep, strong foundation of social values. A robust foundation for inclusive progress.

To cultivate tolerance, we must respect others—even those whom we disagree with or abhor—by cleansing ourselves of the negative emotions of enmity and by adopting a loving attitude toward all. However, it is not possible to radiate love without loving oneself. The Loving Mindset *(Prem Bhav)* is a state of being that is highly conducive for this purpose.

We can acquire this inner state by surrendering ourselves to a figure of our belief—the Guru Tatwa. We could submit to a person, a living being, or an inanimate object—anything that embodies the spirit of our belief. Alternatively, we could surrender to our love for our Guru Tatwa. Surrendering entails strict adherence to the Guru Tatwa's guidance and the expression of our devotion. If we follow this process, we will kindle the Guru Tatwa in our hearts, triggering self-love. As the love for our Guru Tatwa blossoms, the bond between the self and the Guru will grow stronger. Eventually, we will form a composite, spiritual whole with our Guru. Consequently, self-love will be magnified. Happiness will flow constantly and bountifully through our souls.

A person with the Loving Mindset can express love to everyone, even those professing opposing views. They can give the dissenter a patient hearing. They can digest their opinions without jumping to judgmental conclusions. Of course, they may not accept the other person's views if their values diverge markedly. However, they are in a loving state. In this mindset, they are focused on the other person's happiness. In this mode, they will certainly respect their values and opinions. Their words and actions will be expressed with the intention to emit positive energy, provide constructive feedback, and further the other person's well-being. This is how the Loving Mindset will help them convey respect to their detractor.

Respect begets respect. By virtue of the golden rule of reciprocity, they would earn the other person's respect. Of course, there are exceptions to this rule. If the other party is full of inner negativity and lacks awareness or recognition of the same, they may be unmoved by the positive gesture. Even in such aberrations, however, a person with deep self-love would not be deterred from expressing positivity. Impervious to the poison from the infected darts, they would unleash a torrent of love that would overrun the recalcitrant one's dam of resistance.

To conclude, we can develop tolerance by loving ourselves. Through self-love, we can express our respect for the views and values of others. Cultivate this faculty. Feel the happiness of being ensconced in the loving embrace of the Universe.

Question 26

Does It Pay to Be Patient?

Very often, we face a situation where we must make one of the following choices—to wait or to act. Usually, this decision crops up due to exigency or a pressing need. The course of action must be tailored to the urgency of the situation. We may choose to wait for something, or we may choose to take prompt action. Notwithstanding our final decision (to act or to wait), we often feel the pressure to make a decision—some decision—one way or the other. This feeling of being rushed into decision-making affects our satisfaction levels for a number of reasons. It prevents us from being in the moment. It stops us from observing things unfolding at a natural tempo. Most importantly, it hampers our flow with the environment.

Patience is a state of being. It is a mindset that enables one to accepts life on its terms and be fully present with passion in each moment. A patient individual is the one who experiences life as it flows naturally. They enjoy participating in every moment. At the same time, they are detached from the outcome. This definition of patience may suggest that it is an undesirable quality because it detracts from results. This is far from the truth.

No outcome of any activity—be it starting a venture, registering with a dating service, etc.—is ever in our control. That being said, we *can* be in control of the process by controlling our energy. When our thoughts and feelings stay positive, we emit positivity and attract others into our energy field. In turn, others radiate love and enrich our world. As discussed, even if the outcome was undesirable, we would be satisfied because we had detached from it. However, to sustain the flow of positive energy, the initiator—oneself—must be fully present in every moment. To attain this state of being, we must accord greater importance to enjoying time than spending it. This would ensure that our core resource, energy, is utilized more productively and that the outcome is further enriched. Therefore, it is likelier that a patient person would achieve a more favorable outcome than an impatient individual. Here is an example:

The initial followers of Prophet Mohammad (570–632 AD) included the marginalized, destitute, and imprisoned underclasses of Mecca. It was amongst these downtrodden people that the teachings of the *Quran* first took root. However, the powerful Quraysh tribe (Mohammad's lineage) objected to the precepts of the new religion because they were polytheistic and practitioners of idol worship. War broke out between Mohammad's followers and the Qurayshis over differences in ideology, such as monotheism. Subsequently, the Prophet and their flock migrated to Medina and created their settlement. After several years, the followers attempted to re-enter Mecca and engaged in protracted armed conflict with the ruling forces. Mohammad then realized that a prolonged war would alienate potential followers of Islam. He might win the military battle, but he would lose the ideological war. So, he decided to be patient. He would win the war of hearts and minds, he resolved.

In 628 AD, he signed the Treaty of Hudaybiyyah with the Qurayshis. The truce marked an end to the conflict for a period of 10 years. During that period, Mohammad focused on spreading Islam in the neighboring territories. Through his outreach, he was able to attract a huge number of followers. Consequently, the nascent faith of Islam gained significant traction in the Arabian Peninsula. 10 years later, his patience was finally rewarded. Even his Meccan oppressors converted to Islam.

This story illustrates the positive impact of patience on one's initiatives. Notwithstanding this benefit, many people believe that a patient person acts too slowly, often to their detriment. Is this true?

Patience does not necessarily encapsulate a longer wait time. Since patience is a mindset of accepting and enjoying life, a patient person would not act unless they are immersed in every nuance and detail of the activity. This could happen instantaneously, or it could take a longer time. Regardless of the time to act, the patient person lives and breathes every moment of the process so deeply that they can feel the energy tingling their veins. They are so attuned to the energy of others in their environment that they are constantly energizing them and making their surroundings more positive. Hence, they appeal to others. On the contrary, the impatient person is more focused on the outcome of the activity. They are driven by their need to complete it and see the process as a means to the end—a process they could skip if possible. Consequently, they are less concerned about the details of their actions, let alone enjoying every moment of time. Could they energize the environment as effectively as the patient person can? Obviously not.

As a virtue, patience polarizes society. For many people, it is a compelling value. For others, it is an undesirable quality that is associated with stagnation. The conflicting views stem from the notion that patience is an internal quality driving action. People believe that an analysis of the outcome of the action would reveal the positives and negatives of its underlying trait. On this basis, it often appears that patient people take too long to act and achieve sub-optimal results in comparison to the impatient folk. This hypothesis breaks down when we define patience as a state of being.

According to this concept, a patient approach to life leads one to be present in the moment and to engender a balanced set of thoughts and feelings. In turn, this inner positivity spurs a series of actions that create a chain of positive energy. Patience, therefore, yields multi-faceted benefits than just the outcome. This is why it pays to cultivate a patient mindset.

Question 27

Is It Beneficial to Accept All Things?

For most of us, discrimination has become a way of being. There are certain things that we accept warmly. There are also many things that we reject. The objects that we cluster into the accepted or rejected buckets include physical goods, people, living beings, ideas, values, etc. The reasons underpinning our decision to discriminate are complex. However, they are all rooted in social conditioning. Since birth, we have observed the world through colored lenses, tainted with the biases of society. It is like watching a film that is embedded with a continuous stream of opinions and reviews. Is it possible to be neutral after being bombarded by all that noise? Due to social conditioning, we assign weights to different things—'1' for good, '0' for bad. Subsequently, we accept or reject these things.

There are profound consequences of nonacceptance in our lives. When we reject something, we, in effect, refuse Nature's gifts. This is tantamount to slapping Her on the face. Consequently, our negative thoughts, feelings, and actions pollute our cycle of deeds with undesirable consequences. At the same time, we also ascribe a high value to an object representing the opposite in meaning to that of the rejected thing. Eagerly and lasciviously, we accept this counterfoil.

The result of selective acceptance is the birth of lust in our souls. For instance, we refuse to consume an apple because we do not like fruits.

Therefore, we gladly chew on a candy bar instead. As a result, we are denied the nutritional benefits of fruits. This affects our long-term health. On the contrary, if we played favorites with the fruit over the candy bar, we would have missed out on the soul comforts that are part and parcel of confections. Thereafter, we would have felt considerably less joyful. In both cases, our hearts get filled with lust due to our discrimination. The preference for fruits stems from our lust for good health. A desire that compels us to compromise on specific social activities and relationships. Similarly, the choice of candy is due to our craving for sensual pleasures. Thus, discrimination has a personal cost, even when it is centered around a socially-approved thing like an apple.

Lust is a significant barrier to the growth of consciousness because it prevents us from incorporating virtuous practices and observances in our life. Lust militates against the prerogatives of sexual restraint and self-discipline, preventing one from achieving a deep connection with The One. Since discrimination gives rise to lust, it is important for an individual to accept all beings. *Aghor Panth* is a set of practices that enables one to universally accept all Nature's beings—living and nonliving—in their purest forms. The Aghori is distinguished by their face and body, painted with ashes from a cemetery. Aghori rituals were conceived to help adherents unite with Lord Shiva, thereby achieving ultimate consciousness. Here is an example of someone who practiced universal acceptance.

Yogeshwar Krishna was the ultimate Aghori. He accepted all that came in his path of life—from love to war to curses. He never tried to avoid any of these challenges, setbacks, or opportunities. He never attempted to dilute, reject, or question them. Instead, he accepted them in their pure, unadulterated form. Consequently, he experienced tremendous inner churn. Regardless of the pain, he spent his life with a permanent smile on his lips. Consequently, he reaped the benefits of Aghor and attained the highest state of consciousness, i.e., *Shaivata*.

Based on this example, we can see that Aghor Panth provides us with a philosophical pathway to develop our sense of acceptance. This is an important essence for our journey to Oneness. The trait of acceptance helps us to maintain a mental state of attachment with detachment. A fundamental state of being that is absolutely essential for the pursuit of conscious development.

Question 28

Is Materialism in Conflict with Spirituality?

Over the last 50 years, society has become highly materialistic, as it values the satisfaction of desires over inner growth. The acquisition of objects—both physical and intangible—entitles bragging rights over the pursuit of meaning and inner contentment. Today, a lavish culture of consumption has permeated every aspect of the lives of individuals who are regarded as middle class and above. To cite an example, 30 years ago, air conditioners were discretionary items. Nowadays, they are necessities. Household ownership of multiple television sets, air conditioners, and individual possession of multiple cars and phones have become the norm. With each generation, numerous luxury items turn into necessities. This transformation of demand patterns has further embedded the culture of materialism into our consciousness, much to our detriment.

The purpose of acquiring material goods is to fulfill basic needs, such as food, security, mobility, etc. However, due to social changes, i.e., nuclearization of families followed by unitarization, and the hollowing of communities, isolation has become the norm. Consequently, many emotional needs like belonging, appreciation, and intimacy, that used to be fulfilled at the collective level, are unmet. Perversely, the agents of materialism (corporations, governments, and allied institutions) have capitalized on this emotional void by producing a surfeit of goods and services. In the process, hapless people have been ensnared into an eternal web of materialism, which is a tangled skein that has prevented them from pursuing the enrichment of the soul.

When the purpose of consumer goods broadens to fulfilling psychological needs such as fame, social recognition, and belonging, we get trapped in an eternal cycle of desire, expectations, actions, and negative thoughts/emotions. As a result, we turn into hungry wolves, constantly sniffing out sources of self-gratification. Here are examples of people who began their spiritual journey only after forsaking materialism.

Sri Aurobindo Ghose (1872–1950) was an Indian philosopher and nationalist. He is renowned for his views on human progress and spiritual evolution. However, the trajectory of his life, during his first 40 years, belies this characterization. From his birth right up to his imprisonment in Pondicherry, Sri Aurobindo focused on achieving specific material goals—ranging from professional success to political achievement. Educated in the UK, he pursued a career as a civil servant. After graduating with stellar results, he returned to India and joined the State Services in Baroda, where he was appointed as an ICS officer.

Subsequently, he joined the freedom movement and concentrated his energy on various revolutionary activities. Due to his exalted professional status, he was never short of the luxuries and comforts of life.

In 1910, he was imprisoned in Pondicherry. In jail, he was provided with the bare necessities—stale food, water, clothing, and books. Relegated to living in these Spartan conditions, he redirected his mind from materialism to the discovery of a higher purpose. Aurobindo realized that he had been overly attached to many things, including the freedom movement. Thus, he started to detach himself from all these objects of material wealth and ego. This was a crucial prerequisite for his spiritual quest.

This was a journey that yielded many fruits, such as the seminal treatise, *The Synthesis of Yoga*, and the center for spiritual awakening, Sri Aurobindo Ashram.

Tulsidas (1532–1623) was a poet who was legendary for his devotion to Shri Ram. His most famous work is *Ramcharitmanas*. Prior to his spiritual transformation, however, he was a randy lover who was obsessed with his wife's physical assets. One day, Tulsidas visited the Hanuman temple. While he was gone, his wife, Ratnavali, went to her father's home. Tulsidas was not aware of her trip. When he found out that she was missing, he was distraught by the thought of sleeping alone. So, he swam across the Yamuna River in the middle of the night. Ratnavali chided him for this act. She said that if he had been half as devoted to God as he was to her flesh, he would have been redeemed.

Ashamed, Tulsidas left the place and introspected. He realized that he craved a spiritual epiphany more than anything else in the world. Yet, his hunger for physical gratification impeded this inner pursuit. After accepting his wife and respecting her desires, he experienced complete satisfaction in his marriage. The episode marked the onset of his spiritual awakening and the start of a remarkable literary journey, highlighted by the publication of the epic, *Ramcharitmanas*.

These stories tell us that when we are locked in a perpetual state of desire, we are unable to focus on spirituality—our journey of conscious development. The road to Oneness necessitates the practice of attachment with detachment. This is the only state of being that is completely lust-free, even more than pure detachment.

To filter ourselves from lust, it is necessary to turn the negative energy of expectation into love. We can do so by witnessing every moment with passion, thereby connecting with the Ultimate. There are numerous methods of doing the same, Patanjali's eight-fold *Ashtanga Yog* being the gold standard. Irrespective of the path being pursued, it is difficult to attain a blissful state of pure connection if our mind is constantly buffeted by the noisy honks of expectation. Thus, it is imperative for a person to detach from materialism and its concomitant ego before pursuing conscious growth. This is why spirituality begins when materialism ends.

Question 29

What Does It Mean to Succeed?

We live in a world where success is glorified. Every billboard, magazine, television set, or social media platform is covered with images of people who have performed well by social standards. These examples are meant to inspire us to aim higher. Indeed, a large number of us *do* try to follow in the exalted footsteps of the heralded. While some of us reach comparable benchmarks, the majority do not. Thereafter, we experience a swirl of deep disappointment and disgruntlement due to failure to meet expectations. Subsequently, this spiral of inner negativity foments fear and lust—entrapping us in a cycle of adverse intentions, actions, and consequences—preventing us from developing consciousness.

Success is commonly understood as the accomplishment of objectives that align with established expectations. These are metrics such as ideal family life, high household income, stellar academic credentials, impressive professional achievements, and indulgent lifestyle markers. The yardsticks serve the purpose of categorizing people so as to allocate benefits like social recognition and power. These standards exist because it has always been believed that a hierarchical structure of authority is the most efficient way of preserving natural resources and social order. This is why the hierarchy and its allied currencies have been the social norm throughout history.

Notwithstanding the logic of social outcomes, it is undeniable that they do more harm than good.

The currency of social outcomes poisons the soul with lust and perpetuates expectations, instead of filtering barriers. We feel as though we have been forced to scale a mountain that has been chosen for us. It is a journey where we are constantly battered by the never-ending storms of fear and anxiety. A journey where we rarely feel in control. For most of us, this ascent is a relentless struggle with stressful situations. Nevertheless, it is a trek that we cannot quit, lest we want to face the condemnation of society. Even if we were to succeed in the endeavor, we would be immediately presented with more artificial mounds to scale, a series of ascents designed to distance us from our true selves. These man-made travails are distinct from the challenges that Nature poses.

To resolve challenges posed to us by the Universe, such as a sudden personal crisis, we have to remain true to ourselves by acting while being fully present in the moment. However, when we strive to achieve socially established outcomes, such as wealth or power, we feel compelled to go against the grain of Nature and often violate our personal rule book. To attain these milestones, more often than not, we become calculating, utilitarian people. We discriminate between beings—living and nonliving. At times, we oppress them in order to maximize their utility. On other occasions, we compromise on our rule book. Because these actions are driven by lust, their negative consequences linger in our consciousness for eons, stymying the journey of our soul to the Universe's womb. Fortunately, the trap of social expectations can be averted.

We can escape from the pit of expectations by immersing ourselves in the journey of life. In this state, one is entirely focused on the challenge at hand, relishing every moment while trying to resolve it, and staying completely detached from the outcome.

Kapil Dev presented a glorious portrayal of this mindset during the 1983 cricket World Cup. In a crucial league match against Zimbabwe, India was in grave danger of being skittled out for a low score following a devastating spell of seam bowling by the African contingent. However, Kapil Dev approached the challenge with gusto and fearlessness. His heart held no attachment to the trophy. It only throbbed with excitement and exhilaration like that of an explorer who is about to embark on a momentous expedition. Fully present in the moment, he batted with class, panache, and courage, dispatching the Zimbabwean bowlers to all corners of the stadium. Eventually, he scored 175 runs and enabled India to not only win the match, but also gain sufficient self-belief to win the Cup.

Kapil's state of mind is an exemplar of success. It entails experiencing every moment of life like a person who passionately witnesses everything that is occurring. Their enjoyment of the activity is so great that it exceeds the pleasure derived from even a desirable outcome. In this state of being, the heart is perpetually throbbing with the beats of the Universe. The mind has been permanently imprinted with the sights, sounds, and smells of those moments. Thus, it is evident that the cumulative impact of the experience on one's consciousness is richer than the fleeting pleasure of the outcome. Based on this insight, we can now redefine success.

Success is the satisfaction of witnessing every moment in life with passion. This is why you must not chase social expectations. Give your all. Then, *let things be.*

Question 30

Can We Be Happy Without
Owning Anything?

Since birth, we have been conditioned to aspire to own things. These objects include material and immaterial things, even living beings. From necessity items (e.g., soap) to luxury goods (e.g., handbag) to intangible attainments (e.g., fame) to human relationships (e.g., companionship), we have been led to believe that everything in the world can be owned. Our conditioned belief is rooted in territorial rights. Throughout history, colonies of settlers used force to establish exclusive possession over tracts of land. This idea of 'territorialism' outlived those colonial days, subsequently expanding to nearly all aspects of life. Today, our adherence to the concept of ownership is so deep-rooted that we regard every object, person, and nonliving being as a bar-coded water drop in an ocean of resources.

When it comes to the living and the nonliving, ownership is the exclusive right to determine the destiny of a being. The right is manifested by the power to assign access, usage, consumption, or transfer of the being. If you own a being, only you can determine its fate. This territorial concept of ownership is evident in every facet of life.

By preventing athletes from signing contracts with different parties, a council of sports administrators demonstrates ownership over its players. By insisting that his wife seek his permission prior to meeting someone, a husband demonstrates ownership over his spouse. By refusing to allow a neighbor to use her lawn, a resident demonstrates ownership over her property. The forceful exertion of ownership rights has a detrimental effect on one's pursuit of conscious growth.

The sports administrator is buffeted by feelings of anxiety and rage—the same negative emotions that the disgruntled, handcuffed athletes emit into their environment. The recalcitrant husband is forced to deal with his wife's silent disappointment by either compensating her in another form or by oppressing her even further. Whichever route he chooses, he ends up drowning in feelings of negativity. The selfish resident experiences anger when her subsequent request to remodel her garden is rejected by other community members, who were aghast by the neighbor's refusal. In all these cases, the principal characters lose their mental and emotional balance and hurtle into a vicious spiral of negativity. The descent into 'gloomdom' makes it impossible for them to banish judgments, practice attachment with detachment and witness every moment with passion. Therefore, the focus on ownership detracts from conscious growth. Here is an example of a man who renounced the idea of ownership and became spiritually evolved.

Vishwamitra was one of the most respected saints in ancient India. Before his spiritual rebirth, he used to be a powerful king. One day, he was travelling through a village. Maharshi Vasistha, a legendary sage, lived there. He owned a mystical cow named Kamdhenu. Vishwamitra decided to stay in the village with his army of soldiers. However, he did not know where the soldiers would stay or how they would be fed.

Vasistha had solutions to these problems. Kamdhenu produced copious milk in order to feed the soldiers. Astonished by this feat, Vishwamitra became jealous of Vasistha and wanted to possess his cow. He declared that such a magical creature should belong to him, not a lowly villager. Mustering his regal authority, he commanded Vasistha to give up the beast. The latter refused to comply and Vishwamitra retaliated by declaring war. He ordered his soldiers to kill Vasistha and capture the cow. Miraculously, Kamdhenu produced a legion of soldiers that defeated Vishwamitra's army. Exhausted and humiliated, Vishwamitra slunk back to his kingdom. He then learned from sage Vamdeva that Vasistha was a rishi who had achieved supreme consciousness. To defeat him, Vishwamitra would have to acquire special powers by performing intense *tapasya* (penance) to Lord Shiva.

Abiding by the guidance, Vishwamitra became a *Hatha Yogi* to acquire the inner qualities of grit, strength, foresight, and patience. Eventually, he pleased Lord Shiva with his penance and was presented with a set of celestial weapons— arms he could use to vanquish his *bête noire*. Subsequently, he attacked Vasistha for the second time. Once again, he was defeated. Upon introspection, Vishwamitra realized that the consciousness earned to serve a material objective is shallower than one that has been garnered through selfless devotion. As long as he remained focused on the ownership of pride and authority, his spiritual evolution would always be limited. Thus, Vishwamitra realized the futility and destructiveness of his desire to own the cow, indeed, of *ownership* itself. Thereafter, he renounced his throne and all material possessions and embarked on a spiritual journey. Eventually, he became so highly regarded as a sage that he went on to groom Shri Ram and Lakshman in the arts of celestial weaponry, philosophy, and religion. This story shows that we can be happy without owning anything.

What is the alternative to ownership?

Non-possessiveness.

This idea does not mean that we have to share everything readily. After all, there may be people who have malicious intentions behind using their hoard. Non-possessiveness is a feeling of detachment from the beings in one's sphere of ownership.

Take the example of a ball. You have owned it since childhood. If you interpret your role in the life of the object as that of a caretaker, you will say, "Hi, Ball! I am your guardian. My job is to look after you and keep you safe and clean. Beyond that, you are on your own to shape your destiny." By uttering these words, you are reiterating your responsibilities toward the ball. At the same time, you are disavowing your attachment to it. In this mindset, you feel fondness for the object. However, should a situation arise in which you would have to part with it, you would do so joyfully.

A non-possessive state of being is crucial in cultivating a mindset that experiences attachment with detachment. This state of flow enables us to accept things gratefully and to let go gracefully. When we reach this inner space, we instantly redirect our energy from fulfilling desires to worshipping The One. Thereafter, we feel ourselves floating toward the origin of the Universe. This meditative state, achieved without engaging in actual meditation practices, is a state of sublime, supreme harmony.

In this state of being, we realize the universal truth.

We own nothing. Nothing owns us. We are all part of One and the same.

Sign Off

The growth of consciousness is a journey to the center of the self. Unlike a conventional trip, this one has no end. Even after experiencing the Ultimate, you can extend the journey further by diving deeper within yourself. The journey is also one that has no limits. There is no limit to the power of devotion that you can ignite in yourself. There is no limit to the extent of your sacrifice and surrender. There is no limit to your love. The Universe's response is equally unbounded. There are no restrictions on its gifts. No fetters to your destiny. No boundaries to its impact.

Above all, there is no limit to your happiness!

About the Author

An entrepreneur and spiritual leader. A hard-nosed businessman and philosopher. A devoted family man and community stalwart. These usually describe different individuals. Except for Harit Ratna.

He embodies all these qualities and more. He is a man of contradictions who effortlessly floats between the disparate worlds of the rich and the poor, the old and the young, the educated and the uneducated, the privileged and the marginalized and the religious and the atheist. Descriptors aside, his life mission is his defining parameter: The mission to help every human being achieve enlightenment.

Harit Ratna was born in 1976 in the city of Sitamarhi in Bihar, near the Nepal border. After completing his higher studies in Kolkata, he began his career in entrepreneurship. Over the course of two decades, he built a portfolio of businesses ranging from an advisory service to the Agricultural Ministry, from a manufacturing company to a film production house. During his business tenure, Harit Ratna discovered a new facet of his persona—philosophy. Passionate about the growth of consciousness, he began to delve into its various nuances. His immersion led to the development of the philosophy of Oneness and its eponymous foundation for spiritual upliftment.

Oneness is a state of being where an individual is united with the universe at its origin (Yog). In this state, one is free from all attachments, i.e., needs, values, and relationships. Therefore, one can experience happiness on a perpetual basis, not just sporadically. This maximal development of one's inner self, or enlightenment, is the objective of Oneness. The core of the philosophy is that it details one's journey from an unbalanced spirit to ultimate consciousness. This path is described in Harit Ratna's seminal treatise, *Yug Purush,* and its English translation, *The New You.* It is the cornerstone of Oneness (www.onenessindia.org), a Kolkata-based foundation that organizes programs for soul navigation and spiritual alignment. By following the philosophy of Oneness, we can all progress in conscious growth from awareness to awakening to achievement and journey to the center of our Self.